DRAMA GUIDELINES

CECILY O'NEILL
ALAN LAMBERT
ROSEMARY LINNELL
JANET WARR-WOOD

Heinemann Educational Books
in association with London Drama

Heinemann Educational Books Ltd
22 Bedford Square, London WC1B 3HH
LONDON EDINBURGH MELBOURNE AUCKLAND
SINGAPORE KUALA LUMPUR NEW DELHI
IBADAN NAIROBI JOHANNESBURG
PORTSMOUTH (NH) KINGSTON

ISBN 0 435 18670 1

First published by London Drama 1976
First published by Heinemann Educational Books 1977
Reprinted 1978, 1979, 1980, 1981, 1983, 1985, 1986, 1987

Designed by Stella Jackson

Printed and bound in Great Britain by
Biddles Ltd, Guildford and King's Lynn

CONTENTS

FOREWORD

Guide-lines are not guide-dogs. They are not intended to help along those who cannot see. Nor are they tram-lines, laid down to take the skill and adventure out of steering. Primarily, guide-lines require us to ask the question 'Why?' and insist on staying for an answer.

Reaching towards the truth, towards accurate perception of how things are or should be, is often as much a matter of questioning the answers as answering the questions. So I hope the ideas in these guide-lines will not be inertly received. They deserve to be widely discussed, reflected on and reacted to.

It is impossible to experience the work of London's drama teachers without recognising that there are some who are working at the frontiers of their craft. Here, now and in London there are many to learn from. A few of the many speak through these pages. They give us a sense of direction without a sense of being directed.

That is what guide-lines are for. That too is what London Drama does so much to promote. That is why both deserve to succeed.

Peter Newsam
Education Officer, Inner London Education Authority

INTRODUCTION

This book has a very clear message. It is a statement of the objectives of drama teaching by the ILEA drama advisory service. Descriptions of actual lessons, set out in shooting script style, illustrate theory.

Deliberately there is little reference to presentation and theatre — that is, any of the wide range of activities from simple presentations at assemblies to sophisticated productions, CSE Theatre Arts courses, study of texts for public examinations, acting and stage management exercises, and so on. All that is part of our job, essential areas of what is broadly called drama in schools, but in this document we don't wish to add to what is written in the many publications on these topics.

DRAMA GUIDELINES encourages teachers to extend themselves, and to reassess their practice. It urges them to ask themselves a whole set of new questions — before beginning a lesson, during it and afterwards. The main questions, however, are the fundamental ones for teachers in all subject areas: 'What do I hope the children will have achieved as a result of this lesson?' 'Are they achieving it?' 'Did they achieve it?'

The primary source of inspiration for this book is Gavin Bolton — lecturer in drama at Durham University Institute of Education. He has given many sessions for ILEA teachers. It is also very strongly influenced by the ideas and work of Dorothy Heathcote (lecturer in drama at Newcastle-upon-Tyne Institute of Education). In addition the editors acknowledge their debt to John Fines and Raymond Verrier (authors of 'The Drama of History'), Veronica Sherborne, Chaz Hanam, and the many ILEA teachers who contributed to this book in a variety of ways.

As the vast majority of recruits to the teaching profession have received no adequate drama training, local education authorities must accept responsibility for making suitable provision. In the ILEA the main springboard of this provision is through a small team of drama advisory teachers. For more than 60% of their time they remain in the classroom working alongside teacher colleagues helping to improve the quality of education. They run weekly workshops for teachers running right through the year, which are supplemented by shorter and/or more specialised courses at the arts centres and teachers' centres. This document is the distillation of the philosophy they have explored on courses and in the classroom.

Drama as described in this book is the only teaching method stretching right across the curriculum to facilitate and deepen the whole learning process. With personal understanding and communication skills at its heart, it is an essential tool in the teaching of oracy and stands with literacy and numeracy at the core of education.

Geoffrey Hodson and Maureen Price
ILEA drama inspectors

OBJECTIVES IN DRAMA

The long-term aim of drama teaching is to help the student to understand himself and the world he lives in. The drama teacher is trying to set up situations within which his students can discover why people behave as they do, so that they can be helped to reflect on their own behaviour.

Physical, emotional and intellectual identification with a fictitious situation is dramatic activity. This active identification is what is characteristic of all drama teaching, whatever differences can be observed in the aims and structures of individual lessons; it is this *active* involvement and identification with a fictitious situation which is unique to drama. When this activity becomes part of an educational purpose, it is a drama lesson.

A secondary aim in drama teaching is for students to achieve understanding of and satisfaction from the medium of drama, since this is the means by which the primary aim is achieved. But unlike those working in theatre, one is teaching not *for* the aesthetic experience, but *through* it.

Drama in education has altered greatly during the last twenty-five years, and is still changing. There has been a shift in direction from an interest in the personal development of the individual pupil through the acquiring of theatrical and improvisational skills, to the recognition of drama as a precise teaching instrument, which works best when it is seen as part of the learning process, and when it is embedded firmly within the rest of the school curriculum. Drama is no longer seen only as another branch of art education, but as a unique teaching tool, vital in language development, and invaluable as a method in the exploration of other subject areas.

This edition of Drama Guidelines will, we hope, reflect this shift in emphasis. In it, we will be as much concerned with *overall purpose* as with *overall structure*.

Drama in education can achieve the following ends:

1. Drama is to do with human behaviour and relationships, therefore the social health of the group should improve.

2. The individual's use of language should be extended, since drama provides situations where language use arises out of a genuine need to speak.

3. Through drama, pupils can be helped to grasp concepts, face issues, and solve problems.

4. Since drama uses what the pupils bring to the drama from their own experience, it can diagnose what they already know — where they are at in their thinking.

5. The pupils will be stimulated to writing or drawing, within or after the drama lesson, and to reading, observing and researching as a result of the drama.

6. Particular subject areas can be explored, and illuminated through drama. Drama provides access to another perspective on the material, and should extend pupils in their thinking *beyond* what they already know.

In this edition of Drama Guidelines, we are not aiming to give any short cuts to instant and successful drama teaching. Success in teaching in any discipline is not achieved by handy lists of new ideas and novel activities, used once and discarded as soon as their novelty wears off, and still less in drama. By showing the experience of particular teachers with specific aims in actual situations, we

7

hope to encourage others to re-examine their own classroom practice. The descriptions of actual lessons which form the central portion of this document are not intended as models to be slavishly imitated, but have been chosen to illustrate the points we wish to emphasise about the teaching of drama. We hope that the thinking behind each of the lessons is clear, and that the strategies described, although designed to fit particular needs, will prove useful to other teachers in their own thinking and planning.

We do not necessarily expect them to alter their own teaching as a result of this publication, but we hope that they may begin to look at their own attitudes to and objectives in drama, and begin to question *why* they are engaged in particular activities, and what they hope the outcomes of those activities will be. We will be asking them to consider aims and objectives, strategies and evaluation.

Drama Guidelines is in three sections:— Drama in Practice, Lessons, Aspects of Drama.

'Drama in Practice' sets out, as briefly and clearly as we can manage, some of our beliefs about the principles of drama teaching. Statements are supported by references in the margin to a lesson in the 'Lessons' section or to a topic in the 'Aspects of Drama' section.

This arrangement enables the reader either to read straight through, following the argument uninterrupted by illustrations, or to linger over each point, looking up references as he goes along.

DRAMA IN PRACTICE
THE FUNCTION OF THE DRAMA TEACHER

The drama teacher is engaged, not in instructing his pupils, but in creating areas of learning for them, which is a far more difficult task and takes a great deal of time. It is the attitude of the teacher to this task which vitally affects what goes on in the lesson. The drama teacher must be prepared to share the process of learning with his pupils — which, for the 'know-all' teacher, will be particularly difficult to do. The success of the drama lesson will finally depend on the teacher. It is not enough for the drama teacher to provide an initial stimulus, to 'throw a switch' and then sit back and wait for the drama to happen. Too often in drama, there is an assumption that the teacher is scarcely necessary, and that the children are capable of making discoveries and deepening their work themselves. Many teachers are hesitant about intervening in the children's work, in case they interfere with creativity or self-expression. It is often assumed that the greater freedom the children are given, the greater will be the 'creativity' that ensues. But left to themselves, with the teacher merely acting as facilitator by suggesting the context, providing an external stimulus, or commenting on an end product, the children are unlikely to create drama which extends them beyond what they already know, nor are they likely to achieve any significant insights in the course of the drama.

The function of the drama teacher is to challenge, arouse, interest, make anxious, give confidence, co-ordinate achievement, encourage reflection. In any one lesson, he may operate in these or a variety of other ways. No more than the maths or history teacher can he abdicate from his responsibility to assist and support his pupils in their learning.

PLANNING AND CONTROL

Lesson 12
Lesson 5

In planning, the teacher decides what the needs of his class are, and what experiences he wishes them to have in the drama lesson. The teacher can choose the *context* for the drama, taking suggestions from the class, or following-up some subject area which the class are already studying. Within this context, he needs to decide on the specific focus for the lesson — where he is going to start. This focus should be thought through in considerable detail, so that he can be sure it will contain the elements he wishes the children to experience, and that it allows exploration of the wider issues. The focus needs to be sufficiently exact to allow the class a sense of involvement, and to pinpoint the problem or conflict in a *concrete* way.

Once the context is selected, the teacher creates a particular climate in which the learning can take place. He directs the attention of the class, he opens up possibilities, he evaluates what is happening, and judges the right moment for further development of the theme. He needs to be able to use and build on his pupils' contributions, so that the learning may be genuinely shared.

Control is often the most difficult factor in the drama lesson, and one which worries even experienced teachers. Because the conditions in which drama is taught, and the relationship between teacher and class are likely to differ from those of other lessons, the usual classroom controls are not always appropriate. The drama teacher is inviting and encouraging physical and verbal activity, rather than suppressing it. But he must make certain that he is teaching within the limits of his own security, and that he can contain the contributions of his class within a meaningful framework. Equally, his pupils need to feel 'safe' in what may be, to them, an unfamiliar and threatening situation. It can help both teacher and class to be genuinely adventurous and creative if the 'rules of the game' are clearly understood. These 'rules' will vary for each individual teacher, but every teacher will need to ask himself how far the environment in which the lesson is held, the signals he is giving to the class, his own attitude to drama and his pupils' expectations are affecting his control of the lesson. If his aim in drama is merely to give his pupils 'fun', or to compensate for a difficult maths lesson, if his relationship to his pupils is an attempt to be 'best mates', and if he is unwilling to accept his responsibilities as teacher, then he should not be surprised if his pupils do not take him or his drama teaching seriously.

[1] Lesson 1
'A circle has many advantages: a teacher has a total view of the class, but can make quite individual relationships across the circle; there is a togetherness that is not a herd but a unity; there is a stage ready made, and it only needs one footstep to enter it; there is no hierarchy of space.' *Fines and Verrier*

See Teacher in Role and Spontaneous Improvisation & [2] Lesson 4 & Storytelling

[3] Lesson 8
[4] Lesson 14

We suggest that control is most likely to prevail when the class is interested and motivated by what is happening in the drama itself. A great deal of time spent in attempting to achieve concentration by doing nothing but concentration exercises, for example, will not necessarily prove successful, and may pay rapidly diminishing returns. A belief that the activities in which he and the class are engaged are in fact meaningful and significant is the best control device that the teacher can use.

Useful control devices which can be employed in the drama lesson will be identified in the lesson examples, e.g. physical groupings[1], teacher as narrator[2], established instructions which the class recognise, 'still photographs'[3], short exercises and games[4] which promote particular concepts within the drama, physical involvement, slow motion, individual verbal commitment. The teacher need not assume that sensitivity and concentration can never arise out of the drama itself, but must always be worked for directly through preparatory exercises.

OBSERVATION AND INVOLVEMENT

The drama teacher should train himself in observation of the class — its moods, its needs and what it is able to learn. He will become aware of class groupings and leadership, which are often expressed in the physical way the class arranges itself, and class strengths and weaknesses. If the pupils are unable to get easily and rapidly into a circle, for example, they are unlikely to be able to organise themselves effectively in the drama. He will learn to read the atmosphere in a class at the beginning of the lesson, and will not, for example, use 'warm-ups' if the class is already warmed-up to the point of hysteria. He will become aware of his group's ability to co-operate, plan, solve problems, and make decisions, and his knowledge of his class will indicate to him *what they need to learn through drama.*

Total involvement from the entire group may never be achieved in any subject, but in the drama lesson lack of involvement is immediately apparent, and constitutes a threat to the security of the teacher and the co-operation of the rest of the class. The class which is kept extremely busy in non-stop physical and verbal activity may all *look* more involved than a class which is slowly working its way towards the group understanding of a problem, but it can be misleading to judge the level of involvement on external appearance. Since the level of attention of individuals within the class will vary from moment to moment, the teacher need not be put off by the apparent occasional lack of involvement of particular pupils — the rest of the class will probably not be affected, and the lack of interest may be temporary. It may be possible within the drama to challenge individuals who seem uninvolved and their commitment may be gained. The teacher's awareness of the lack of involvement of a particular individual or group should not reach the stage where he is aiming his teaching solely at those pupils, unless their lack of commitment is preventing any growth or development in the drama.

Lessons 6 & 7

11

BEGINNINGS

The beginning of the lesson is vital — it sets the pace and tone of what is to follow, and decides the level of commitment of those involved, especially the teacher. It will establish the context, and make clear to the pupils what is going to be expected from them. If the beginning is to be effective, it must be planned in great detail, including the physical organisation of the class and the actual words to be used. The economical use of time is vital in the drama lesson, especially in the secondary school where teachers are often limited to a bare thirty-five minutes with a class. Too often, the first part of the lesson is used for warm-ups, relaxation, exercises and games, and the drama is postponed indefinitely. Some of these elements may be necessary to the success of the lesson, but they may dissipate the attention of the pupils, create an atmosphere of extreme excitement, and reveal the teacher's uncertainty about how and when to begin the drama. If the beginning of the drama is clear and well-planned, it will give security to both teacher and class.

When the beginning is correctly set-up, the teacher will not fall into the danger of over-planning at the expense of the pupils' needs. If real belief is to grow in the pupils, the teacher must be prepared to hand over the initiative to them as soon as possible. The contributions of the pupils within the drama lesson must be given real importance. By picking up statements and signals from the children, and selecting those which the teacher feels will provide a fruitful area of further growth and inquiry, real learning may take place. Even destructive and idiotic offerings from individuals must be faced seriously — frequently this kind of contribution is merely a kind of testing of the teacher — does *he* really believe in what he is asking the class to do? Sometimes, these contributions can even be made a meaningful part of the action. Well-meaning but inappropriate statements can often be supported by the teacher and turned to good use in the drama.

It is important not to anticipate what the children may offer, and not to have preconceived notions about the limitations of their ability to handle complex ideas, language and situations.

SELECTIVITY AND BELIEF

All effective teaching is selective, and drama teaching demands a high degree of selectivity, in gesture and language. All the signals, verbal and non-verbal, which the class receive from the teacher should be consistent. This need for selectivity is revealed especially clearly when the teacher is working in role with the class — one of the most basic and effective strategies which is available to the drama teacher. In role, the teacher is not acting, but is using a precise selectivity of gesture to reveal attitude.

Teacher in Role & Spontaneous Improvisation

When the teacher works in role, he multiplies the number of facilitations open to him. He can extend his pupils within the drama process, and challenge them in a way which might not be possible as teacher; he can be aggressive, he can support a minority view, he can move the drama on, he can present alternatives. Role can be a very efficient way of finding a concrete focus for the lesson. It allows the teacher to affect materially what is happening, to make it significant, and to elevate it to a higher plane of experience.

The quality of the children's belief will depend on the teacher's ability to believe fully in the situation himself. Drama must never be done with tongue in cheek — it will not work, and will be a denial of the truth.

Many teachers demand instant belief from their pupils, and are disappointed when their class is unable to achieve this, yet, unconsciously, the signals which they themselves are transmitting may be denying that belief. Where a teacher's usual mode is friendly, or even facetious, it may be very difficult for him to move on to any other level. His pupils will have learnt from him that drama is fun, perhaps even a joke, and though both teacher and class may enjoy themselves, and the social health of the group may be excellent, it is unlikely that any deep *intrinsic* learning will take place as a result of the drama itself.

Teacher in Role

SLOW SOLUTIONS AND RE-ENACTMENT

Growth in drama comes with slow solutions. All action and no pause for thought is unlikely to produce anything but superficial work. It is important in drama to 'build the culture' — the background from which one is going to ask the pupils to make their decisions and solve the problems which arise. One should try to 'stay with the moment' — to deepen the experience — to make what is to come more significant by postponing the action. It is necessary to build concern and urgency. The action is slowed down, and the conclusion of the action may be indefinitely postponed, but the emotional pace is increased. It is not the point of 'conflict', which is often thought to be essential to drama, but the preparation for the conflict, which is likely to provide the learning experience.

Too often, pupils are required to imitate or demonstrate dramatic moments, instead of experiencing them. For some children, re-enactment may be an important experience — therapeutic, social or artistic, but the teacher must be aware of why he is asking his pupils to re-enact something. What does he want them to gain from the experience? Re-enactment can leave one free to savour feeling, and to focus on form, since decision and action are not required. But this concern with form may descend to a need to get the story right — the emphasis is placed on the sequence of events, and not on the inner meaning of the narrative. Far from enriching the child's understanding, there is danger that the initial experience of the story, poem or incident is merely diluted by subsequent action. Story presents a completed narrative, and may be limiting unless the teacher is skilled at using *implications* of the story — perhaps to build a new narrative rather than to re-enact the old. There can be ample room for exploration within a situation in which much is already known, and this exploration is a realisation — a bringing to life. Since it is the situation which is being explored, there is no demand for histrionics, or for audience response, but for greater penetration of the situation and its implications by the individual and the group. To dramatise is not to imitate.

LANGUAGE

The part played by language in drama is crucial: movement, silent ritual or mimed tasks may all feed into the drama, but it is the pupils' use of language which will determine the depth and intensity of the work, and will provide the teacher with the best means of assessing the experience.

Lessons 1, 2 & 9
Some Ways In

Speech in a make-believe situation is more accessible to the pupil than narrative speech, since the situation is already represented, and the speech remains in context. The talk does not remain in isolation, but is embedded in the situation, and is subject to inter-action and modification from the rest of the group.

The best way of helping the young child to talk, and therefore to learn, will be by encouraging his participation and exploration of talking situations. The usual response of the pupils to the teacher in the school may be a limiting one, but drama provides both teacher and pupil with the opportunity of tapping an enormous variety of situations that are not encountered in the usual pupil-teacher relationship.

If our aims in drama are to increase the competence of our pupils in language use, we should ask ourselves the following questions about the tasks we set in drama:

1. What kind of language resources is the task calling on?

2. How can we use language to explore the situation and its possibilities more fully?

3. What is the relationship between the verbal and non-verbal parts of the lesson, and can one feed into and strengthen the other?

It is possible to set up drama which will provide the children with the following opportunities for language use:

Some Ways In
Prepared Improvisation

Reporting on past and present experiences, both real and imaginary.

Lessons 8 & 13

Informing, instructing, and explaining.

Lesson 7

Arguing, convincing, persuading, justifying, defending.

Lessons 4 & 15

Planning, predicting, projecting beyond the immediate situation, deciding.

Lessons 2 & 5

Logical reasoning, presenting pros and cons, coming to conclusions.

Role Play

Negotiating and mediating.

Lesson 15

Adapting to particular models of language set up by the teacher or the group.

Lessons 1 & 11

Developing new uses of language arising from the demands of new situations.

The pupil can test the effectiveness of his use of language through drama, and increased competence in language use should come about as a response to opportunity combined with motivation. It is from successful experiences with words that a pupil builds up his resources. Language must continue to grow roots in first-hand experience, and drama can provide a variety of experience which might otherwise remain inaccessible.

QUESTIONING

Lesson 4

Lesson 2

Lesson 5

The drama teacher needs to become a skilled questioner — to use questions to focus on a particular situation or to open up the universal implications of a particular situation. This questioning can work *within* the drama — to test commitment, to deepen the thinking level of the children, to challenge assumptions, to move the drama on, or *outside* the drama itself, as part of the reflective phase of the lesson.

Too frequently the teacher uses questions merely to check facts, and neglects the opportunities which skilful questioning can provide for stretching the children in their own thinking. Teachers should become aware of their own use of questions — to what extent do they merely evoke the obvious response, or even the Yes/No answer, and how often do they genuinely support the hesitant pupil, challenge the superficial response, and guide the class towards new areas of learning? With the insecure or uncertain pupil, the use of the Yes/No question can allow him to make an individual commitment to the work, and may encourage him to a more adventurous contribution later. Questions can also be used to feed in information in an economical way, to test where the class is at in its thinking, and to lead the class in its reflection upon the work.

REFLECTION

It is essential to provide the opportunity for both teacher and class to reflect together on the drama experience. The handling by the teacher of this reflective phase in the drama lesson requires as much skill as the setting up of the drama itself. It is the way in which we reflect on experience, and generalise from it, which ultimately causes us to modify our behaviour. Reflection can take place within the drama, in actual discussion at the end of the lesson, in written and art work arising out of the drama, in developing a dramatic statement in which the insights achieved during the drama are shared with others, or in further reading and thinking. It is the reflection on the experience, as much as the experience itself, which leads to understanding. Often, it is during the reflection upon the experience that the teacher can begin to evaluate the effect of the lesson upon individual pupils, and the level of their involvement and interest.

Lesson 1

Lesson 5

Because we have been conditioned to equate drama with 'doing', and because reflection comes at the *end* of a period of activity, it is very tempting to skimp this most important ingredient of the lesson. We need to discipline ourselves to plan a substantial time for reflection, and *never* to sacrifice this in the excitement of action.

ANALYSIS

One should constantly re-assess one's approach in drama, and avoid over-employing particular tactics, so that they become stale. The kind of comfortable, familiar lesson, in which both teacher and class can anticipate almost exactly what is going to be expected of them, is unlikely to lead to much learning. Spontaneity, flexibility, the sense of exploration and discovery, should be maintained. There is always a range of strategies open to the teacher, and he can select those most suited to the needs of the subject and the group. Each strategy makes a different kind of demand on the teacher's planning, and on the class, and each will make a different kind of learning happen. The teacher needs to decide what he wants his class to experience, and why.

After the lesson, it may help the teacher to cultivate an analytical approach to his own work, if he selects *some* of the following questions, and answers them in terms of his lesson.

These questions have been adapted from a series prepared by Dorothy Heathcote for her students.

What kinds of activity did I set up for the class, and how did I do this? By requests, pleading, choices, orders?

What kinds of questions and statements did I use?

Did I succeed in signalling my intentions clearly to the class, or was there confusion in my thinking?

What was my function in the class? Did I take a role, enquire, insist, monitor, direct?

How did I divide the lesson — doing, talking, reflecting, testing ideas, exploring, making, arguing, proving, negotiating, challenging, researching?

Did I use the right strategies in order to achieve my intentions?

Did I change direction during the lesson? Why? What effect did this have?

Did I slow down the action sufficiently for it to matter, and to allow the class time to build a belief in the situation?

What kind of activities did the class initiate? What do I think of the class, and vice versa?

Was I able to read the signals the class was giving me?

What was the attitude of the class, and did it change for better or worse during the lesson? Did I have anything to do with these changes?

How did the class affect me, and vice versa? What things threw me, and how did I recover?

What things drove me in the lesson? Time, pace, certain children's interruptions?

What changes occurred in the class groupings? How and why did they happen?

What kinds of learning occurred in the lesson? What learning areas were planted for the future?

EVALUATION

A drama lesson is often evaluated solely on externals — did what the pupils were engaged in *look* right? In drama in education, one is attempting to assess an inner experience and not merely the external manifestations of that experience. One may begin to assess the lesson by looking at such factors as the atmosphere in the room, the quality of the pupils' response, the level of their contributions and commitment, and the quality of their reflection upon the experience.

To discover what the pupils have taken from the drama experience is not easy. Those pupils who have been actively involved in the lesson will reveal the quality of their response and the level of their thinking in their verbal contributions to the drama. But many of the class may be unable yet to operate effectively in a group situation, or may not have had the opportunity to indicate actively the level of their involvement. Through written work which is part of the drama, or which arises out of it, it may be possible for the teacher to discover what their response has been. Art work, and discussion can also give insight into what the 'inner experience' has been for individual members of the class. A teacher who knows his class well will be able to identify areas of growth for individuals which have occurred as a result of the drama — perhaps an improvement in the ability to relate to others in the class, to suspend disbelief, to make significant contributions to the work. If a teacher can recognise the elements in a lesson which have helped to create a meaningful experience for the class, he can build on this success in future lessons.

In the drama lesson, two kinds of learning can take place:

The first may occur because the drama lesson itself is so different from other lessons in the curriculum. This very difference in atmosphere and activity can lead to improved relationships with the teacher and within the group. There may be intense activity, involvement, vitality and enjoyment to be observed. This should not mislead the drama teacher into believing that this is happening as a result of what is going on in the drama itself, rather than because of the special conditions and the nature of the activities in the drama lesson.

The second kind of learning happens as a result of the drama itself — the insights which have been gained, the elevation of language which has occurred, the understandings which the group have reached.

Lessons 1, 5 & 16

The first kind of learning is easier to achieve. The importance of it must not be discounted, nor should the drama teacher remain satisfied with achieving only this kind of learning.

LESSONS

The lessons in the following section have been chosen, not because they are totally successful examples of drama at its best, but as workmanlike drama lessons by a number of teachers in which there is some degree of achievement. The structures and methods used within the lessons will, we hope, illustrate most of the points contained in the first section of the book. We repeat that it would be unwise to attempt to imitate or reproduce these lessons; however, the insight they give into the different teachers' thinking, planning and use of strategies, may prove useful to the teachers who read them.

Although they cover Infant, Junior and Secondary work, the lessons have not been arranged in chronological order. Some subject areas may prove more fruitful with one age group than with another, but many themes can be used effectively across a wide range of ages. For instance, lessons 15 and 16 use the same context and starting-point with very different groups. There is no reason why Infant drama should be kept firmly at fantasy level, or Secondary Fourth years should be restricted to drama based on social problems.

Most of the lessons described here include the strategy of the teacher in role, with the class working as a whole group, but contained within this broad framework are examples of half-class groupings, small groups, pairs and individual work. Mime and physical activities are seen as playing an important part in the drama, and language use, in interaction, discussion, decision-making and reflection, is vital.

Since these lessons come from a number of different sources, there are within them inevitable differences of style and emphasis. However, we hope that the format we have used will give some consistency, and will provide a coherent framework for individual lessons.

LESSON 1

SIR DOMINIC

4th Year Juniors; 12 boys; school hall

Lesson time: 45 minutes

Objective: To test whether understanding of a moral dilemma can be achieved more effectively through drama than through a narrative. This lesson was part of a project on Moral Education.

The teacher introduces class to the kind of drama he is offering. He gets their interest and builds their confidence. He introduces the idea that he will be in the drama, in role.

The teacher builds atmosphere and significance.

CIRCLE — very useful shape for the drama.

The TEACHER IN ROLE. A ritualistic and formal atmosphere is established.

Teacher input.

The teacher re-inforces the significance of each offering.

He is able to test each child's involvement and belief, through their verbal and physical commitment and selects 'Sir Dominic' accordingly.

This is the third use of RITUAL in the lesson, and focuses the attention of the class absolutely.

2nd teacher in non-speaking role.

The teacher explains to the boys that in the kind of drama he does, they will need to pick up signals immediately; there is no time to plan in advance. He suggests they have a short practice. He speaks to one boy: ' "Two packets of chips, please." Where am I?' 'A fish shop.' 'Who am I?' 'A customer.' 'Good.'

To another boy: ' "Now then, son, what's your name? What are you doing out at this time of night?" Who am I?' 'A policeman.' 'That's right.'

The teacher tells the boys that the next one will not be so easy. It is set far back in time, and they will need to go slowly. It is going to be a very serious play.

The teacher asks the class to sit in a circle. He solemnly takes his seat among them, and begins in role:

'Stand before your king. I welcome all you brave knights to my court. I know you have travelled many miles and done many brave deeds. Let each knight take his sword from his belt and give the usual salute — To England!'

The boys salute.

'This is no normal day. On this day I shall select one chief knight, and give him the title of Sir Dominic, the chief above all other knights. It will be very difficult to choose the best among so many brave knights. Be seated. We have often discussed among us the qualities of a knight — his courage and chivalry and loyalty. I would like each of you to tell me some true story of your strength and courage. I need only hear the beginning of each man's tale. Who will begin?'

In turn, the boys tell a story. Already, their language has been affected by the formality of the situation, and the growing tension. At the end of each tale, the teacher says: 'That is a good tale; it pleases me well, Sir Knight.'

When each boy has made a contribution, the teacher says: 'I know your brave deeds, and already I know whom I shall choose. Now I would like you to demonstrate your strength by raising the throne on which you have been sitting above your heads. These thrones are not made of ordinary wood; it is possible to raise them swiftly, but the real trial of strength is to see how slowly they can be lifted.'

Each boy slowly raises the chair on which he has been sitting over his head.

'The time has come to choose. I shall walk around the circle, and where my finger stops, there is Sir Dominic.'

The teacher walks slowly round the circle *twice*. There is real and mounting tension and excitement.

One boy is selected. 'This is Sir Dominic, the chief of all my knights. Take your place on the right hand of your king.'

The new Sir Dominic is toasted by the company. During this ceremonial, a letter is delivered to the king, who reads it aloud. It is from a beggar who is waiting outside the castle gate. In times gone by, he has helped the king. Now, he is in desperate straits, and begs the king's assistance. The king is furious at this interruption of the festivities. He turns to Sir Dominic.

'Sir Dominic. This is your first task. I imagine that you will know how to deal with such a man.'

Sir Dominic goes out of the hall. Outside, another teacher is seated in a huddle on the floor.

The king becomes impatient. 'Why is he taking so long? Would the rest of you know how to deal with such a person?' The boys think that they would. One boy, who seems to feel that he would have been a better choice for Sir Dominic, begins to wonder what is happening. The king sends him to see. He leaves, full of confidence, but returns rather abashed. 'He won't go away.'

Another boy offers to go. All the boys return, and confess that they have been unable to get the beggar to move. The king is furious. 'You have failed in your task — you the chief of all my knights. You are not fit to be Sir Dominic.' To another boy, 'Take this man and set him to work in the kitchens.'

2nd boy asks eagerly, 'Who'll be Sir Dominic now?'

King: 'Certainly not you. You also proved yourself unworthy of the task.'

Then, out of role, 'Right, that's the end of the play.'

The reflective phase:

The teacher then examined the implications of what had occurred with the class. What kind of king was he? Was he a just king? What did he expect of his knights? Among the questions put to the boys were the following:

Questioning and reflection. Making sense of the experience.

1. Normally beggars would never dare to write to the king. Why did the beggar do this?

2. How do you think Dominic felt when he saw the beggar? Why did he feel like this?

3. If Dominic had known what would happen to him, would he have treated the beggar differently? Why?

4. Did Dominic fail in his duty towards the king?

5. Did Dominic do right towards the beggar?

6. Was there anything else he could have done?

7. Was the king right to punish Dominic?

8. Think of a situation today where the main character is faced with a similar problem.

In this lesson structure, in order that the pressures from the king and the rest of the group might be balanced by a solid reality so that the dilemma was a real one, a second teacher was used, as the messenger and the beggar. Both roles were silent, and could be taken by an older child, a student or a colleague.

Strategies:

The use of Role by the teacher — a formal authority role, using elevated and formalised language.

2nd teacher in passive, non-speaking role.

The story of a brave deed — individual verbal commitment in narrative form.

Test of strength — ritualised physical activity.

Choice of chief knight — ritual.

Letter — moving on the drama.

Discussion and reflection outside the drama.

LESSON 2

A VILLAGE UNDER THREAT

1st year Juniors; 30 children; classroom

Lesson time: 4 lessons, 25 minutes each

Objectives: To encourage the children to make decisions concerning the behaviour of the group, and then to question the value of these decisions.

The idea of a 'village under threat'. The 'village' was a complete mystery but the 'threat' was going to be some 'large footprints'. The teacher had the idea of some sort of monster, etc. but the culture which the children produced would have made this quite useless — the threat obviously had to be to the culture they had built which was so jealously guarded.

The children were rather apt to get carried away with the traps and what lurked in them! The teacher brought them back to the question of what was it that they had that was so special that it needed to be so well guarded. Traps otherwise were a red herring.

The children's idea of the role of Mr. Know-All was a very lucky one!

The children did it entirely by themselves. Their class teacher was disappointed with it as a piece of art work, but the drama teacher was pleased with it as a pictorial document which contained to the smallest detail everything about the village.

The teacher feeds in the idea of meetings of the village to try to deepen the commitment to the ideas. But they anticipate this by bringing forward the thief.

The 'thief' was the one non-English speaking child. The teacher was worried that he was being picked on but he seemed to take it well. In role she could make sure he was not excluded as a punishment for his 'crime'.

Another factor had to be fed into the play. The teacher was going to call a meeting and tell them she had had a letter from another village — but again she was beaten to it.

1st Week

The children gather around the teacher on the 'gathering around' chair. She tells them that they are all villagers living together in the same village, but that is all she knows. By answering her questions they build up a picture of the village. After a short while the teacher does not have to ask questions and the children offer ideas freely. They build up a picture of an 'arcadian' society — self-sufficient, peace keeping. The whole village is surrounded by a large wall — why, asks the teacher. The children say it is to keep out intruders. The children then enter into long discussions on the type of traps they use to keep out those who come to destroy their village. The teacher points out that therefore their village must be very special — why? The children answer that others are jealous. The teacher asks why? They find this difficult to answer. She hopes this will become clearer as the work progresses and the village starts to be 'built'.

The first lesson is almost at an end and all they have done is to build the culture of the village. The children have decided that the leader of the village is Mr. Know-All. The teacher asks if she can play this role. She asks the children to come next week having decided who they are in the village and what is the job they do.

2nd Week

The children gather around the chair. They have made a large picture collage which is a visual list of all the information they put forward about the village the week before. The children have also decided on a series of signals using percussion instruments to give signs — 'Mr. Know-All is coming'. 'Call for a meeting'. 'Strangers are coming'. The picture is given a dominant position from now onwards behind the chair as an important possession of the village.

The children tell the teacher who they are, and what their job is.

The teacher asks them to sit by themselves around the hall. She 'talks them through' the beginning of the day — getting up and going out to begin their work. The children begin the improvisation and the teacher in role as Mr. Know-All goes round questioning each one as to the way their work is going, ordering clothes, etc. The children are interacting with each other in role.

Two children bring forward a third who they say has been caught stealing. The teacher decides that there must be a meeting. One child who has decided to be the teacher's assistant makes the signal for the meeting to be called. The idea of the circle for meetings and the speaker standing is introduced.

Mr. Know-All asks why the child was stealing — because he didn't have any animals or machinery. What can we do about this? They decide to make him a loan of same — to give him a time of six months' 'probation' — there is also a charge that he is in league with some from another village. Other general problems of the village are discussed.

3rd Week

The children are told three months have passed. It is now Winter so things are harder for them. Short discussion on what problems they would have. The children begin their day again, only this time the situation is slightly different. The assistant brings Mr. Know-All a letter from the leader of a nearby village. He says it is very important and they must have a meeting. The signal is given.

When the children are in the circle Mr. Know-All tells them that a stranger is being sent to the village from a neighbouring village. He wants to know whether they are going to receive him or not. The decision must be theirs alone. He leaves the circle and goes some way off. The children discuss and then decide to vote. They are against the stranger coming — but then the teacher is told that they have received a letter which says that the stranger will come even if they say 'no'.

There was some unease at first but a few of the children soon took the initiative.

According to what the children decided the problem for the next week was either — the stranger/or — who would take over from Mr. Know-All who was getting old.

4th Week

When the children come in they are asked 'Can we make our circle?' The teacher walks slowly around the circle. Then she asks 'May I enter?' When given permission by the children she sits on the floor with them, completing the circle.

The stranger tells them her people are in trouble — without food, squabbling among themselves, not sharing, etc. Everything is different in their village — will they tell her their secret? They discuss between themselves then decide to vote. They vote to tell the stranger some of the secrets. They tell her that the happiness they have is caused by a special liquid which is sprinkled on them when they are children. They decide to give her some for her people, also machinery, etc. Some will come to her village to instruct the people in farming — the children will be allowed in their school, etc.

The teacher in a 2nd role. She asks in a natural way as she wants the children to accept her in a new role — hence the walking round the circle and the sitting on the floor.

A mode of speech has grown up. The children are telling the teacher 'You must —' and the teacher in role is answering 'I will remember and I thank you'. The children then bring her all the things which they are sending back to her village. She takes her leave of them. She then re-enters the circle as Mr. Know-All. They discuss how else they can help this village.

This became very ritualistic.

Back to the chair.

Strategies:

Teacher provides context (the village), children add detail.

Teacher in role first as Mr. Know-All, second as the Stranger.

Art work — to establish detail.

The work of the village — mimed physical activity and verbal commitment.

Letter — moving on the drama.

Discussion in role.

LESSON 3

THE MAGIC BOX

1st and 2nd year Infants; 36 children; classroom

Lesson time: 45 minutes

Objective: To encourage the children to work imaginatively together, using their knowledge of Nursery Rhymes and Fairy Tales.

The teacher tells the children that she has a magic, invisible box. Inside is some magic dust. If you sprinkle the dust on you, you will go to the Magic Land.

What is the Magic Land like?

This formed a large part of the lesson.

The children build up a picture of a land which has houses that speak, trees that walk, witches and wizards, birds that can carry you, ponds of magic water that change colour etc.

The teacher was looking for a 'role' she could play. She wanted an authority role so that she could challenge the children.

The teacher asks them who rules in the Magic Land. The children decide a witch called Isabel, who lives in a castle. The teacher says they can't go to the Magic Land because she has lost the key to the box. The children suggest places it might be. 'Under your bed.'

'But I haven't got time to go all the way home to look.'

Very theatrical but it served to catch the children's attention.

One child suggests looking in the 'hidey-hole' behind her. The teacher looks and finds it there. She makes quite a business of fitting the key into the keyhole and slowly turning it. Cries of 'It's turning' from the children. The teacher opens the lid and says the magic dust is safe inside. She asks them who wants to go to the Magic Land. They all do.

The teacher asks them to close their eyes while she sprinkles the dust on them. She then moves away from them and tells them to open their eyes and they are in the Magic Land.

One of the children says 'Look! I can see one of the trees moving over there' — 'And there's another one over there.'

The teacher rushes up to them and shouts 'What are you children doing in my Magic Land? How did you get here? Do you know who I am?'

'Isabel the witch.'

'The Witch' talks about how the children have got there and asks what they can see in the Magic Land. The children ask to see the Witch's Castle. The Witch says yes, if the children will draw her a beautiful picture of the Magic Land because as the Witch is getting old she is finding it difficult to see things from a distance.

The children go to rush back to their desks.

A useful control device.

'The Witch' quickly casts a spell that makes the children move in slow motion.

They move slowly back to their places and draw their pictures while 'the Witch' moves around asking them about their pictures.

The Witch says the pictures are so beautiful that she can see her Land clearly again. She takes the children around her 'castle' (the classroom) and then it is time for the children to go 'home'. The children say they can get back to their own land by drinking the magic water. Again the children close their eyes while 'the witch' gives them some magic water to drink and when they open their eyes they are back in the classroom.

Strategies:

Introductory discussion.

Teacher in authority role.

Magic spells — as starting and finishing, and as control devices.

Art work — leading to verbal commitment.

LESSON 4

THE SAD KING

6—7 year olds; 15 children; classroom

Lesson time: 35 minutes

Objective: To encourage the children to negotiate verbally and on a serious level.

The children are told the beginning of a story. There is a king who is very sad. He is the loneliest king in the world. The people who live in the village close to his castle never see him, as he spends all his time shut up in his castle. Although the villagers are very poor, they are very happy. One day, they are all summoned to the castle. They are a bit frightened, but prepare themselves to see the king.

1st teacher as NARRATOR.

One part of the room established as village.

The children move to another part of the hall, where the king receives them, and asks them to sit 'in the proper circle'. He tells them that because he is unhappy and they are happy, they must return to their homes and bring back their most prized possession. He does not want things which are merely valuable, but the thing which they prize most. He sends them home. The children go back to the 'village'. They discuss what they will give to the King.

2nd teacher in role as king. An authority figure, challenging and threatening.

1st teacher as questioner.

The teacher tells them another bit of the story. 'There is one woman in the village who is even poorer than all the others. She has nothing to give the king. The only thing she possesses is her precious baby.'

1st teacher as narrator.

The villagers return to the castle, bringing their gifts. The king asks, 'What gifts have you brought me?' Each child brings his gift to the king, who questions him about what it is and why it is precious to him. Among the contributions are a family bible, a wedding-ring, an ancestral sword, a pet, a favourite dress, a dictionary.

2nd teacher uses RITUAL to build significance, and reinforces the children's contributions.

At last the king reaches the teacher. 'What have you brought me?' 'Nothing.' 'Why not? Has she not got something to give?' 'Yes, her baby,' the children reply. 'You must all return home and bring me the baby.'

The villagers go home, and discuss what they can do. They know that the woman cannot part with her baby. Several volunteer to try to persuade the king to change his mind. He refuses to do so, and is quite sure that he can bring up the baby just as well as its mother.

An understanding of the different nature of this 'gift'.

The mother and all the villagers return to the king. He demands the baby. The children argue with him, and he asks them to explain why the mother is necessary to the baby. They do so, very convincingly, and at length he agrees to allow the mother to keep her baby. And because the villagers have been so kind to him, he promises to help them all.

2nd teacher as questioner, and Devil's Advocate.

Mother remains silent to allow children to negotiate with the king.

Assessment

This structure uses two teachers, but only the 2nd teacher is really in role. The 1st teacher functions almost entirely as teacher, since her role as mother to the baby is almost totally passive and silent. This lesson stretched the children in their thinking (about what was their most precious possession) and about the relationship between mother and child and its special quality, and they were put in the position of having to make their thinking clear to a fairly unfriendly outsider. The lesson suffered from some over-complication, because of the two teachers, and, because there was no opportunity of follow-up work, it had to be brought to a rather contrived ending, in which the king suddenly became reasonable, but it remained a meaningful experience for the class.

Strategies:

Storytelling to establish context.

1st teacher — narrator, and in passive, almost silent role.

2nd teacher — formal authority role.

The giving of gifts — ritualised physical activity and verbal commitment.

Discussion within the drama.

LESSON 5

THE INDIAN CHIEF

Upper Juniors; 30 children; school hall

Lesson time: 2 lessons, 40—45 minutes each

Objective: To use drama as part of a school project on the North American Indians.

The teacher's advance planning included the following:
1. That he would be working in role.
2. That his would be the authority role (initially), i.e. the chief.
3. That the lesson would be about the conflicting ways of life facing the tribe, i.e. hunters into farmers. (He would some-where need to build up the old ways so that the change might mean something.)
4. He would need a long initial discussion with the class to gain security with them. This section lasted for 10 minutes.

Some initial embarrassment was overcome by stopping them and letting them tell friends what they were doing: this helped those children who couldn't immediately think of an activity.

What is important here is not *ACTING/MIME SKILLS* but the commitment and concentration brought to the task.

The teacher stands apart from them. 'My people I have been to see the President as you have asked.' Stressing this should prevent the 'we didn't want you to go' response. It wasn't given enough weight here and the teacher had to work against such a response to make his initial points.

Introducing a simple *RITUAL* which slows down the pace of the lesson and builds belief through its seriousness.

At this point the teacher abandons his original plan, i.e. the change in the life style and its resultant problems. There is strong opposition from a small group who want either to break away or become leaders, so the lesson focus now changes (see opposite).

1st Week

The children gather round the teacher who explains that today they are going to make up a play about Red Indians. What do they know about the tribes, their culture, their history?

The play will start in an Indian Village: the teacher asks if he may, for the moment, be the Chief of the tribe. The kind of activities to be found in the village leads from this discussion to the start of the play.

The children move to the centre of the hall: they each take one of the activities listed in discussion. They work individually and the teacher stresses the care they must take in their work for the whole tribe depends on the group effort for its survival. The teacher allows this to continue for several minutes, encouraging and praising, and then explains that when he next talks to them he will be the chief of the tribe.

Teacher in role enters with a treaty signed by the US President and himself. He has been to Washington as had been asked by his tribe and agreed to these terms of peace. The tribe must gather in council to hear the terms of the treaty.

The class discuss the treaty: they are led to look at the implications behind the terms of peace, e.g., they will need to become farmers and abandon their ways as hunters. They must give up any rifles they possess and, in the council, they are asked to lay these down as a sign of their good intent. The chief shows them a map of the lands that will be theirs.

There is disagreement in the group. Some will accept the treaty, others criticise the chief for signing it. The chief says they must decide what to do. He will leave them to make their own decision and meet with them later. It seems that most of the group will go with the chief but there are five who oppose his authority. This is a matter of great concern which must be resolved. The villagers return to their work: the chief will call them to a council on the next day.

The teacher again gathers the class round him. They discuss the reasons why the tribe found it hard to reach agreement. They know that the next lesson will be concerned with the threat to the chief's authority.

Strategies:

Introductory discussion.

Teacher in authority role.

The work of the tribe — mimed physical activity.

Giving up their weapons — ritualised physical activity.

Treaty — visual focus.

Discussion in role, discussion and reflection outside the drama.

2nd Week

The teacher talks with the class on the issues raised by the previous lesson. This is a very short session since he gauges the mood of the class to be ideal for starting — there is interest and enthusiasm.

Teacher in role calls them straight to a meeting. The chief has decided to look for a successor since he has no children. He knows that his people will no longer follow him without question as in the old days.

A long section follows relating to the old days and the traditions of the tribe. The teacher, still in role, uses it to reinforce belief in the culture of the tribe and to increase commitment. At the centre of this section is a complicated passage on the ways in which we hunt the buffalo: the teacher uses it as a very controlled movement activity within the context of the lesson theme.

The Council is then called on to discuss how we elect a chief: what are the qualities we need in such a man? (Loyalty, bravery, cleverness, goodness, etc.) From the discussion come 3 ways in which a chief may be chosen and the council is asked to vote on these. They decide that a candidate must spend 6 days and 6 nights in the mountains without food and shelter: if he survives he will show himself both strong and wise.

Those who want to be chief tell the others why they think they should be. They are told that they will soon be sent on their test of survival. It didn't happen here but at a subsequent time the new chiefs acted out their 6 days in the mountains. The rest of the class observed them and asked them questions on their return before making their choice.

The lesson ends with discussion, out of role, in which the teacher and class talk through the main points that have arisen in the lesson, e.g. what are the qualities of leadership?

Strategies:

Teacher in authority role.

The buffalo hunt — mimed physical activity.

Discussion and voting in role.

Discussion outside the drama.

New lesson focus:

— what are the qualities of a chief?
— how do we elect him?
3—4 minutes.

Questioning here about: —

(a) weapon making
(b) tepee building
(c) ceremony

Ways around *ANACHRONISM* have to be found by the teacher: a knowing nod is sometimes the only response needed.

Much of this concerned itself with hunters keeping to down-wind of buffalo!! This took a very long time to unravel and was worked out in movement.

The discussion is slow: proposals are questioned by the teacher. No easy answers are allowed.
Other suggestions were:—
1. He who had killed most buffalo.
2. He who was most skilled at archery, riding, etc.
The suggestion voted for was offered by a child who had made very little contribution up till then.

They observe what happens and comment on what is done and not simply on how it is done since acting skills are not the prime concern here.

LESSON 6

A RAILWAY STATION

4th year Secondary; 19 girls; drama room

Lesson time: 55 minutes

Objective: To get a difficult and unco-ordinated group to work successfully together.

The teacher has prepared in advance a pack of cards. Five of the cards indicate that those who draw them are a stable part of the environment. The remaining cards indicate that the drawers are passing through the environment for a short time. The cards are drawn face-down with no pre-knowledge. Further cards could be drawn, if required, to indicate age or sex.

Teacher's strategy — to break with previous environment and initiate lesson.

Class enters. Quiet pop music playing. A few dance for a few minutes while the register is informally taken. Music off.

Group awareness develops.

Class brings chairs into a circle with the teacher. A simple orientation game is played.

General discussion about railway stations as a setting for drama.

The teacher explains that she has chosen an environment for a 'happening' in which everyone will become involved by the use of a pack of cards. The teacher has chosen a railway station.

Station sound effect record is played.

The teacher reads a cub reporter's account for his editor of a day spent on Victoria station from 5 a.m. until midnight.

By fortunate law of chance the hard core of four is broken up. Two are among the five who are part of the stable environment — the station — two have drawn 'passing through' cards.

Cards are produced and drawn. Time to discuss how the station is to be set up. It is decided that the five 'stable' cards will indicate workers on station. Ticket office, cafe, porter, paper stall, cleaner.

Everyone else has drawn 'passenger' cards. (One of these, very lethargic, chooses to become permanent on station as a dosser. Lies on two chairs from then on. Accepted by others in this role. A bad attender anyway, this is the first time she has shared the class activity in any way.)

Teacher is station announcer. Operates sound effects. Announces the time of day.

The day on the station begins. (Some of the class have now chosen further cards to decide their sex and age — others have decided for themselves). Episodic dramas of the day follow, stimulated by the account that was read. One of the lively four has chosen to be blind. Everyone involved in improvising quite well — even the timid ones.

Care of the blind. Conditions of work — loneliness — pressures of life in big city discussed briefly.

Assessment

This method worked with this class in that the group ceased to be abused and threatened by the four domineering characters and everyone was involved. When this 'ploy' is used again it may be that the four will engineer a way around the dictates of the cards. This lends itself to the choice of many environments: an island, an ocean liner, another planet, a hospital, life after death, heaven, hell, 'Outward Bound', 'Huis Clos'.

Strategies:

Newspaper report — establishing context.

Prepared cards — providing information and identities.

Sound effects — providing atmosphere.

Announcements — providing atmosphere.

Discussion outside the drama.

LESSON 7

BUILDING A WALL

5th year Secondary; 22 boys; drama studio

Lesson time: 75 minutes

Objective: Drama work based on an examination text.

The class has read 'One Day in the Life of Ivan Denisovitch' by Alexander Solzhenitsyn. The objective is to extend their understanding of the underlying situation, without 'acting prison-camps'. It is decided to isolate two main ideas — Deprivation and Interdependence — and concentrate on these.

1. Since the boys are comparatively well-fed and warm the deprivation is going to have to be something different.

2. The normal hierarchy of the class is one of size and race. Large West Indian boys dominate the smaller Asian boys.

The Studio is set up beforehand. Two desks at one end of the long rectangle of this dark room. Two large bags of plastic offcuts (cardboard boxes or other rubbish would do) are placed by the desks and two long drama-blocks, up ended, divide the width of the Studio into three open spaces.

Atmosphere deliberately gloomy.

The class assembles outside. The teacher chooses the large 'stronger' boys as 'Zeks' (slave labour). Each one is issued with a cheap Guy Fawkes mask with the eyes almost entirely filled in leaving only a pin-hole for safety. (Blind-folding them would be nearly as good). This is the deprivation.

Three smaller boys are chosen as team leaders. (No masks.)

Two smallest boys are the checkers. (No masks. Issued with pencil and paper.)

The teacher acts as guard. (A watching role.)

The teacher in role as chief guard. Unhelpful but not belligerent. Refuses to talk to Zeks, only to team-leaders.

The class enters the room. The teacher explains that checkers are to sit at tables and issue blocks to the three teams of Zeks who will build 3 walls with them. The team leaders are to give all the orders. Masks are on no account to be removed. The first team to complete its wall successfully will have first break. The spaces must be entirely filled. The walls must not fall down.

Instructions are left deliberately vague but issued in a very authoritative way.

First attempt produces chaos. Blind Zeks stumble about. Checkers issue blocks indiscriminately. The walls fall down. Team leaders blamed for inefficiency. Checkers pressurised when blocks give out.

No interference. The teacher waits for right moment.

The guard whispers to checkers to call in all the blocks and devise a new system of distribution.

More frustration is fed in by refusing to allow Zeks to remove masks even while they wait for the mess to be sorted out.

There is a good deal of fumbling but finally a very over-elaborate but fair system is organised by checkers. Everyone seems happy and work begins again.

Masks are very uncomfortable. Zeks get restless. Work proceeds. Leaders now more efficient but still under pressure from teams. Walls grow quickly.

Guard suggests to checkers that they measure walls. Guard obtains long ruler. Frustration-level really high. Everyone is longing to give up. By sheer chance, one space is found to be 8 inches smaller than the one next to it. This is obviously unfair. The checkers themselves — becoming bolder — order walls to be dismantled and the space evened out. Finally walls are finished and re-checked. Checkers are satisfied. Team-leaders allow masks to be removed. Great relief. Collapse of all the 'strong' Zeks.

The teacher notes that there is still plenty of time and she may have to employ delaying tactics.

This is an unplanned development which could have produced a riot. It does not and guard is not needed.

Discussion

A long discussion follows the break. The boys easily follow the parallel between the drama lesson and the book. The teacher queries the lack of aggression in the class. The boys are not sure if it is due to the memory of the story or not. They admit their normal aggressiveness but will not admit a

The teacher as teacher.

31

reason for today's mildness and submissive attitude. The teacher does not pursue this too far in order to avoid loss of face on the boys' part, but intends to come back to it. Nobody comments on the 'size' hierarchy although the qualities of their leaders are discussed, as well as the need for some sort of hierarchy with rules. The nature of their dependence on the system is also discussed.

Because the boys are tired after the experience, the lesson finishes early. They help to clear up. Many of the masks have been broken (stamped on), some spare blocks are found, hidden away. (An enterprising Zek?) Nobody admits to knowing anything about this theft. The ethical code of the under dog has been established and recognised.

Strategies:

Teacher in supervisory role as guard.

Class divided into teams, with team leaders.

Building the walls — physical activity.

Discussion and reflection, relating drama to text.

LESSON 8

EXPLORERS

1st year Secondary; 30 children; classroom

Lesson time: 1 hour

Objective: The use of drama to give another perspective on the theme of discovery, which is being used as part of a project in an integrated curriculum.

The children gather round the teacher, who explains that they are going to do a play about exploration. They discuss the kind of people who would be useful on an expedition exploring unknown lands. The children provide a useful list, including hunters, map-makers, zoologists, scientists and anthropologists.

The teacher enters in role, and says she is a Government agent, and that they have all been accepted as members of the expedition which will explore the vast new Government purchase of land. A map is displayed, which corresponds to the Louisiana Purchase. Most of the map is blank, but it shows some rivers, forests and mountains, and indicates the presence of some native tribes.

In turn, each member of the expedition explains in role what special knowledge or skill they possess, and what their job will be on the expedition. Some will study native tribes, some have medical qualifications, some are botanists, and so on. Each contribution is received seriously by the teacher, and the importance of each job is re-inforced: 'The expedition will be relying for its food on skilful hunters like you.'

Now each member of the expedition prepares what he is taking with him. They must only take what they can carry themselves. They are asked to assemble at the dock, to board the boat which will take them upstream on the first part of their journey. As they assemble, they are questioned about their possessions.

It is time to go on board. The teacher asks if there is a photographer present. One girl volunteers, and arranges the rest of the class for a photograph. They are asked to 'freeze', so that the picture can be taken, and during the next few moments, the teacher talks them through their journey upstream, to the point at which they disembark, and civilisation is left behind. Then she asks them to gradually change their pose (as for another photograph), to show how they might look and feel different on their arrival.

A base camp is established, and the group are told that each evening they will gather together to report on the day's discoveries. The explorers set out individually on their first day of exploration. The teacher stresses how careful they must be, and asks them to remember everything of interest which happens.

Soon, most of the class are actively engaged in various 'exploring' activities. Some are working in pairs or groups. Two boys, who have been rather uninvolved, are fiddling with the taps in a sink in the corner of the classroom. The teacher calls all the group together, and asks them to report on their findings to the others. There have been many discoveries, several of which could be used as a basis for the development of the drama. One of the boys who have been playing with the taps claims, facetiously, that he has found water. At once, the teacher challenges him. Is it safe to drink? How has he tested it? Was he foolish enough to risk the lives of his companions by recommending that they drink this potentially dangerous water? In the face of this hostile questioning, the boy is unable to remain flippant, and justifies himself by inventing a complex series of tests which he claims to have used on the water.

Of the many ideas which emerge from the reporting-back session, the teacher chooses the one which she feels will provide the most fruitful development for the drama. A group of girls have found a native baby deliberately abandoned in the forest, and have brought it back to the camp. The next section of the lesson is spent in discussing whether it is best to return the baby to its tribe, replace it in the forest, or keep it. The children attempt to understand why the baby might have been abandoned. Many of the class wish to keep it, but

This list of occupations forms the basis for the children's individual choice of profession later on. It could have been listed on the blackboard.

A VISUAL FOCUS to help the class by suggesting some features of the unknown land.

Even minimal contributions are accepted, but when the teacher feels that the pupils can be extended further, they are closely questioned about their skills and qualifications. This section takes a long time, but there is considerable concentration and interest.

Here, listing their equipment might be a good idea. This commits them to certain possessions, and helps to build reality.

This is an excellent CONTROL DEVICE, and is also useful for 'moving on' in time or space.

The teacher moves among them, listening and observing. She has not planned beyond this point, so what happens now is crucial.

A comment designed to be flippant, and destructive, causes him to be 'put on the spot' within the drama. He has to think quickly in order to extricate himself. From now on, the class has his entire attention. This is also a useful lesson for the rest of the class.

LESSON 8

The teacher as Devil's Advocate.

This work can link with reading the diaries of real explorers, and researching the travels of Lewis & Clark in exploring the Louisiana Purchase.

realise the danger they may cause to the expedition if it is discovered. The teacher recommends strongly that the baby should be left to die in the forest. She claims that it is not their responsibility, and that their first duty is to the expedition.

The team return to their tents for the night, knowing that in the morning they will have to take a vote on the fate of the baby.

In the last ten minutes of the lesson, the class are asked to write the log or diary of their first day of exploration, to be sent back to the Government. They may list or draw the things they have discovered, and describe what has happened that day. Many choose to include the dilemma of the baby, and write down what they think should happen to it.

The exploration of America provides the context for this drama lesson, but the learning area which is opened up by the end of the lesson is the decision they must make about the baby.

Strategies:

The teacher in role.

Preparing equipment and exploring — physical activities.

Stating occupations and reporting back — verbal commitment.

Group photograph — control and 'moving on'.

Map — visual focus.

Written work — to consolidate what has happened.

LESSON 9

EARTHQUAKE

4th year Juniors; 27 children; classroom

Lesson time: 60 minutes

Objective: To attempt to explore the effect of natural disasters on individuals and communities, using a theme which was already being studied geographically.

The teacher reminds the class of what they know about the subject already, and explains that they will be tackling the subject through drama. The class choose to be a community living in South London, decide on individual characters and occupations, and set to work. The teacher moves among them, as a member of the community, and talks to them about what they are doing.

The teacher allows the class to choose whether they wish to work with his leadership or without him. They choose his leadership. The role he plays is close to that of teacher.

When they are established in their roles, the teacher, as a news-reader, announces that an earthquake is imminent. People are instructed to collect their families, to leave buildings and pets, to listen for further bulletins and to avoid panic.

Teacher's role changes to that of newsreader. This is a controlling authoritative role, in which the teacher can choose which information to give the class.

Chaos results, and realising that this is unlikely to prove constructive, the teacher interrupts the drama for discussion and assessment.

In discussion, the class examine the implications of their roles, and their possible reaction to the news bulletin. Their previous panic is now seen as un-realistic. They return to their occupations, this time emphasising detail in their mime and characterisations. The news bulletin is repeated.

The teacher comes out of role and leads the discussion as teacher.

The reaction is uncertain and confused, and the teacher once again feels it necessary to stop the action. In discussion they decide that they should make for open ground, and they elaborate the details of their various roles. They return to their occupations, and after 'freezing' for a moment of silence and concentration, the drama continues.

The teacher had anticipated that a leader might emerge at this stage.

The community gather on Blackheath, and after a second news-flash about the approaching earthquake, the teacher gives instructions to ensure the group's safety. A small group of boys decide to remain near their newly acquired house, others find a derelict hut which could provide warmth and shelter. Food is collected and it is decided that this should be shared. Some groups sing to keep their spirits up, while others negotiate the sharing of food and radios. These negotiations unite the class as a whole group again.

The teacher becomes part of the group once more, and hands control over to the children.

The teacher, as one of the community, feels the first tremor of the earthquake. The desks and tables under which the class have been sheltering, overturn, the children spread out and fall, apparently dead.

There is considerable increase in belief and tension. The teacher moves the drama on.

A discussion follows, and it becomes clear that although the class have not worked in this way before, they have been very absorbed, and have worked together with sympathy and spontaneity.

Strategies:

Teacher in role — functioning almost as teacher but within the drama.

News bulletins — to provide information and move the drama on.

Work and food-sharing — mimed physical activity.

Building shelters — physical activity.

Discussion outside the drama.

LESSON 10

VOLCANOES

1st and 2nd year Infants; 36 children; classroom

Lesson time: 35 minutes

Objective: To use drama as an approach to a topic which is being studied in class.

An important 'sounding out period' which helps the teacher to know where to place the drama.

The class were used to doing movement lessons in the hall but had no experience of classroom drama and therefore this process was important.

The children have learnt about Pompeii.

Little response therefore concrete 2nd question. *TEACHER IN ROLE.*

At this point a young class will tend to offer many incongruities which the teacher must handle carefully so that no offering by a child is just dismissed but somehow worked logically into the play.

This discussion formed a large part of the lesson, with the teacher pointing out the implications.

The teacher talks at some length to the children to find out the extent of their knowledge on the topic and to add to it.

The teacher asks them if they would like to make a play about volcanoes.

She explains how she will start the play and the children will find clues in what she says that will help them to decide who they are and what has happened. To help them she begins two 'plays' which stop after about two minutes, then they talk about the play that has started, who they are, what they feel is happening, etc. The teacher then says that the next play will be longer than the others.

The teacher moves away from the group, then walks slowly back to them.

'I've just been to look — but the village has gone. The volcano has destroyed it. We're safe here on this hillside. What are we to do?'

'Did anyone manage to save anything?'

Some children say that they have some food with them. There is not much so it is decided to put all the food together and they choose two people to be in charge of it and cut it up (one child has a 'knife') and share it out at meal times.

They decide they are hungry and so they sit in a circle so that everyone will have a share of the food. One child says that he has been given 2 portions of food, so the giving out of the food is stopped while the children discuss whether the 2 in charge are doing the job properly. They are given a warning and the children tell them a better way of handing out the food so that it will be fair.

After they have eaten the teacher asks them what they are going to do for shelter for the night. It is beginning to get dark and it will begin to get colder during the night. One child says he knows the hillside and where there will be a cave, large enough to give everyone shelter. The teacher then asks the class what they plan to do. The children say they must think about settling in a village.

Do they want to stay together? Do they want to rebuild the village on the site of the old one?

The children decide to build their village on the hillside where they are. What are they going to build the houses of? They decide they will need water so one child goes to look for a stream she thinks she has passed.

How are they going to farm the land? The children discuss different things. They could make the tools they would need etc.

The teacher finishes the lesson by retelling in story form what has taken place during the play.

Strategies:

Introductory discussion.

Teacher in role — unspecified but within the drama.

Sharing food — mimed physical activity and verbal commitment.

Discussion within the drama.

Story used to re-inforce achievement.

LESSON 11

PRECIOUS METAL

4th year Juniors; 25 children; school hall

Lesson time: 90 minutes (including break)

Objective: To examine the reasons for emigration.

The teacher asks for the agreement of the children in working on this new project. He has chosen to start the work in a village, a village to which all belong. He has also chosen a specific date in history: it is 1900. The village is in Poland. The class checks an atlas, but the exact geographical location is not, for the moment, important. The teacher now begins to establish the details of the village from the contributions of the group. It is the children who decide on the occupations and trades, the laws and organisation, and the physical layout of their village. The teacher sifts and collates the agreed information by listing it on a large sheet of paper. He draws a map of the village, working only from information provided by the group. The children are then asked to choose their trade from those listed. The teacher also chooses an occupation (farmer), and asks that *initially* he may be village elder. The children agree. This section lasts 30 minutes, and is followed by break.

The teacher begins the next section by asking some group members to talk about their task in the village. He then asks the group to show him the village at work. As teacher, he observes, comments on the nature of the task, and supports the commitment which is beginning to grow. He explains that he will enter the action with them in the role previously agreed on.

The teacher, in role as village elder, calls the group to the weekly meeting (agreed on beforehand) so that they may discuss any problems that may have arisen. The villagers organise their meeting in the church and the elder joins them. One of the matters discussed is a shortage of metal to supply new axes for the wood-cutters. It is thought that new axes can be bought when the next visit is made to the neighbouring town, but one of the fishermen says that he has seen some chunks of metal at the river bank. It is thought that these also might be used. The meeting ends and the villagers return to work.

In this next section of the lesson, the metal found at the river by two of the boys begins to create an increasing interest among the rest of the class. The teacher observes that much of the physical activity in this section centres on the discovery. He calls the group together, as teacher, to discuss whether this discovery is becoming important in the story. It is, so the teacher develops the theme by moving into another village meeting. The following points are made by the group.

(a) That the metal has only been there for 2 days.

(b) That it is rich man's metal, and it is unlike any metal the villagers have used before because they are poor.

(c) That it is shiny and precious. This information is supplied by one of the villagers who used to work as a silversmith in the town. The rest of the group accepts his word.

(d) That it might belong to the rich man in the nearby big house.

(e) That problems may arise because the villagers are poor and may be suspected of stealing the metal.

The villagers are taken to the river bank by the fishermen. The metal is handed round and inspected. Carefully concealed under clothes, it is brought back to the church. The elder asks for each villager in turn to say what is to be done. The majority think it must belong to the rich man who lives nearby and that

---

The teacher had planned in advance a detailed outline for the lesson, but abandoned this as the lesson developed. He had not previously worked with the group and was working against a time limit.

He explains the nature of the project but gives little information about the outcome of the migration. This may forestall any attempt by the group to reach the 'end of the story'.

The teacher imposes the locale, and the date. All other details are supplied by the class. The teacher can sort out any factual inconsistencies if he feels this is necessary. The drama experience is what is important here: historical inaccuracies can be dealt with later.

Mime is used as an introduction to the drama. The children work individually and those who find difficulties are encouraged. Commitment is more important than accuracy.

The class have had limited experience in this way of working with another teacher.

TEACHER IN ROLE as elder. He felt the need of this authority role initially, but planned to relinquish it to other members of the group as the lesson progressed.

The teacher had planned a second meeting at which he would introduce an edict from the government ordering the people to give up the land. He expected that the rest of the lesson might develop as a protest against this. But what was beginning to happen seemed to have far more potential. It had engaged the commitment of the group. It had become the children's play, and the teacher abandoned his original plan.

The teacher begins to 'slow down' the drama process. It is important that the class tackles *this* problem without coming up with a host of other 'incidents' which may only weaken the central problem by providing instant solutions.

A careful, repetitive and ritualistic placing of objects in a box.

The teacher selects a new learning area. Should the gold be returned to its probable owner, or kept for the benefit of the village?

A *PRACTICE* situation is used to slow down too rapid narrative development. The intended action may seem impossible when it has been practised and discussed, but an alternative course of action is still a possibility. The teacher can also assume another role without having to interrupt the lesson to explain that he is now going to be someone else.

it should be returned to him. There may be a reward. Others argue that it should be used after a safe interval, or taken to the town and sold. The elder asks if any of them know what the rich man is like. A few claim to have met him. The elder suggests that it may be very difficult to convince him that the metal has been found and not stolen. He says that he will pretend to be this rich man. He will see how well the villagers can come to the big house and put their case. The lesson ends with this encounter being set up as a *practice* situation. The class decide how they can enter the house; how the meeting will be set up and what they will say.

Assessment

The lesson moved far away from the teacher's original plan, but gained greatly in commitment, areas of possible exploration, interest and excitement. It is likely that these qualities might not have been present in such a degree, if the teacher had ignored the way in which the lesson was moving, and had insisted on doggedly sticking to his original theme. A very dramatic situation was becoming apparent to the group: the teacher's 'dramatic situation' was apparent only to him, and he might have had a hard fight to gain a comparable degree of interest from the class.

Although the original planning has been abandoned, the teacher's responsibility remains just as great. He must now make sense of what is being offered by the children, and by slowing down the action, find in this new direction a learning area as valuable as any that he had initially foreseen. The next lesson may now explore the 'villagers' relation to the 'landowners'. The theme of people leaving the land *may* draw much from this avenue of exploration.

Strategies:

Establishing the village — the background against which the drama will take place, including: listing trades, making laws, housing, transport, map-making.

Work — mimed physical activity.

Teacher in role.

The meeting — for discussion and decisions within the drama.

Practice: useful for trying out situations and testing alternative directions for the drama.

LESSON 12

BIONIC MAN

Infants. Vertically streamed group; 30 children; school hall

Lesson time: 75 minutes

Objective: To take what the children say and use it in the drama

Children, sitting on floor to listen, are asked what they want to make up a play about and told that they can have as many choices as the teacher has fingers on one hand. They must choose wisely.

Making a contract with the children that this is their play, also using a limiting device to avoid shouting out.

The choice is made by talking about the subjects given and then asking for a show of hands. The subject finally chosen is a favourite television programme about the Bionic Man. The children tell the teacher that he can 'smash down walls, jump over houses and whirl people round by their arms when fighting.' The boys in the group are already using belligerent gestures as they speak.

This may seem like time-wasting but helps to gain co-operation of all the children.

They are asked whether people are afraid of this man. They say 'yes, because you can't kill him because of the wires in his arms that make him strong.'

The teacher feigns complete ignorance in order to get the children to clarify what is important to them in this choice. This also gives her a chance to think, as the subject seems rather unproductive.

'Would he be able to whirl *you* around?'

'Yes, and smash down this hall.'

This cue is taken up and amplified. The children can act together and the Bionic Man can be kept well outside the building. No child can go around smashing things up and being invincible as this will bring all drama to an end in no time at all.

Further discussion follows. The children suggest a place called Iropya which is their country. At this moment an interrruption takes place which affects the whole of the rest of the work. All the girls are to have a dental inspection! It will take quite a few minutes. The boys will then follow. The girls are led off.

Change of direction. Boys and girls are separated.

The teacher asks boys to arrange some chairs in a large circle to mark out the boundaries of the kingdom.

Boys come into the centre. The teacher commends them and points out that they can now guard their country well. She tells them they are fine soldiers, to build such ramparts. When dismissed each soldier will stand behind a chair and this will become his guard-post. The teacher salutes and dismisses the soldiers. They take up their posts.

There is too much equipment in the hall and the teacher wishes to concentrate the attention of the children. It is also a through-way to other classrooms.

When all the girls have returned, the teacher, still using a more formal language, shows the girls how well guarded they are and what magnificent troops they have. When the word is given the soldiers will march out of the hall.

A more formal language is used.

The girls are drifting back.

The boys march off to their dental inspection. So great is their pride that they return, as if from special mission and quietly take up their guard-posts without being told.

Meanwhile the girls are left. They establish what the country is like and begin to prepare food, since the soldiers will return and need a good meal. The teacher questions each one in detail. 'What are you making? Is the cake iced? What have you for the soldiers? Is there ice in the drink?' etc. She also tastes everything to see if it is perfect for the soldiers who have such responsibility for their safety.

The line between an imaginary country and the reality of the hall is blurred and remains so.

When the boys have all returned they share the food but remain on guard. They are asked if they wish to leave their posts but say that they are not tired. They now act as if they were heroes! They have seen no sign of the Bionic Man.

There is a deep gravity in this section.

Belief is growing. Time to move on to the next stage.

The teacher, still speaking formally, says that she knows that there is a message for her from the Bionic Man. She will go to the door and listen to the message. She returns and says that the Bionic Man is angry. The children ask what he will do and make suggestions about how they can deal with him. Guns are no good, they will have to bargain. What can they give him to keep him from

This imaginary person is coming nearer and is more like a giant.

smashing down the wall? Because there are some children who do not speak English in the class, discussion is not easy for them. They prefer to follow the others.

This is quite a good discussion. The teacher is not needed.

The teacher suggests that each one should offer his most precious belonging. Children bring their objects to be inspected. Previously established poverty is forgotten. Jewels, gold etc. are brought out, because the word 'precious' has different connotations to such young children. One boy brings his small pistol and much is made of how valuable a weapon is to a soldier. The teacher says that tools of this sort are always important. Her most important belongings are her knitting needles. Children ask if she is poor. She says yes — then one girl says that she could knit a hat for the Bionic Man.

Indiscreet use of word 'precious' leads to rather a false situation. This is a wrong turning. The teacher wants to retract from this, she changes role slightly and becomes less of a negotiator and more 'one of them' in order to take up the suggestion offered by the boy with the gun.

Pace is increasing. Activity breaks out all over the kingdom. Children move more purposefully within the circle.

She will need wool and everyone will have to help as time is short. Some soldiers round-up some sheep and shear them. Spinning wheels are got out and the wool is washed, spun and knitted. An imaginary trolley is brought in to carry all this knitting, also the valuables, which some children collect in a sack; the teacher is the only one who has no jewels. One girl offers to contribute for her. The boy with the trolley is asked if he is brave enough to wheel the trolley to the door where the Bionic Man left the message. Everyone watches nervously. Even this brave man looks over his shoulder as he returns.

Time to slow down again. (Nearly play-time.)

A meeting is called. Everyone sits down. Two boys still refuse to leave their guard posts, so remain on guard. The teacher broaches the subject of what would happen if their offering were not sufficient. The children offer more 'treasure' which they say they can dig-up. There is little reality in their suggestion. They have no idea of values but they have negotiated well never-theless.

Reverting to teacher role (and standing up, away from discussion) beginning to end, slowly, to bring down the level of involvement.

The teacher decides to leave that subject for another lesson. She says that at least the Man seems to have left them alone so far. They have done well. Can they do one more thing? Put the chairs away and get ready to go out to play.

Realisation that the experience was very real and that some of it is still lingering.

The lines between play and reality are still blurred. Some children drop pretence at once, but others give teacher a 'drink', a 'huge hunk of cake' and a 'necklace'. One child says 'I think I can hear the man coming.' The teacher suggests that this will be a good reason to stop and go outside. The play is over now . . .

Physical and emotional relaxation.

A very quick game is used to break the atmosphere. The children relax their formal attitudes and become 'Class One' again.

Strategies:

The teacher is not in a specific role, but functions within the drama as messenger, questioner, supporter of the children's contributions, and negotiator.

The children's choice of subject-matter is taken as the context for the drama.

Guarding the kingdom — physical activity.

Preparing food — mimed physical activity.

Giving gifts — verbal commitment.

LESSON 13

OLD PEOPLE (1)

3rd year Juniors; 25 children; school hall

Lesson time: 1 hour, 50 minutes

Objective: To make the class aware of, and sensitive to, the problems of the elderly.

The teacher is going to work with the class in making up a play about old people. He knows only how the play will start but nothing beyond this, so everyone will have to take some responsibility for creating this play. Everyone will have a part in the play including the teacher.

The teacher continues with a discussion focused on the problems of old people: what are the ways in which they most need help? Do they know any old people living near? Are the children's grandparents still alive? What are their particular problems?

The teacher is now ready to start the play in role. He moves away from the group, seated as they are in one corner of the hall and explains that when he returns he will speak to them as a person in the play.

Teacher in role welcomes group to this, the first meeting of a newly established voluntary agency for helping old people. He explains that he has been appointed director of this agency. He understands that the group must have seen the newspaper advertisement seeking volunteers: they will go out into the area and help the elderly in their own homes.

He outlines (with a map and diagram drawn on board) the most needy cases in the area; exact details of the nature of help needed are not yet known. What can be done by this agency? After some discussion the director leaves the meeting to come up with its own plans. He will be in his office (a chair at the side of the hall) when they have produced their ideas.

The children (working without the teacher) come up with the following:

(a) home-visiting and helping to carry out tasks that the aged might find difficult.

(b) fund raising schemes (sponsored walks, a jumble sale, a fete, part-time jobs).

Each of the ideas is challenged by the director as to its practicalities. He suggests that since the problems may be pressing, the home-visiting scheme should be the first to operate.

Each member of the group (in pairs or singly) is assigned to one of the households mapped on the board: he/she will be responsible for visiting that house, for preparing a 'case history' of the occupier and for helping in whatever way seems needed. This section lasts 40 minutes and is followed by a break.

The teacher, out of role, recaps on the first session. The play will start again when the group comes to its second meeting — but the members must come prepared with a case history of the person(s) they are visiting. They must compile a list of information e.g. name of OAP, age, housing conditions, special problems, etc. or it might be helpful to simply map out a plan or drawing of the house they are visiting.

The class has not worked in this way before: the teacher introduces a series of brief exercises to introduce the idea of the teacher taking a part (i.e. the teacher in role).

The teacher places great emphasis on questions. He does not accept the facile response — the easy solution will not be acceptable in the play when he will challenge the class to defend and justify their actions.

The teacher explains
(a) his role
(b) the role of the class
(c) the initial situation.
It is important that all are in the same play.

Teacher assumes an *AUTHORITY ROLE* — not far removed from his usual one.

A *VISUAL FOCUS* is used to aid theme development.

The initial discussion continues here and in much the same way the children begin to offer suggestions in role.

The teacher reinforces the significance of each offering and selects the contribution that aids development of the theme. His seriousness indicates his commitment is now being tested by the few who are not yet ready to accept the rules of this 'game'; he also provides a support for those who are risking a contribution. This is a crucial stage in building the belief in the lesson.

The teacher has planned to this stage in the lesson: he knows, however, that the next phase will be for the class to do some planning (in this case a home-visiting scheme, but it may, for example, have been about the planning and preparation of a jumble sale, etc.)

This section could have been more effectively done in role.

The teacher uses written/drawing work as an integral part of the drama lesson: it helps provide a focus for the individual's ideas.

LESSON 13

The group meets in a *CIRCLE*. The meeting is a lengthy one and some contributions are not given enough time for development, but each offering made is once again given significance by the teacher. There is now a deeper level of commitment.

The teacher stresses that this is a *PRACTICE*, each group is left to work out its own methods: there is no right/wrong way since at this stage ideas are still being tried out.

Care and slowness are the important things.

The potential for drama lies in this section of the lesson: the group must be confronted with an issue and work together to a solution which is not easy: here individual members are presented with problems but the solution comes too easily and is in no way a shared emotional experience.

The group reflects on the experience of the lesson. Has it helped promote in the children a deeper understanding of the problems faced by old people?

At the second meeting the teacher, once more in role as agency director, hears some of the case histories, questions and guides the meeting to consideration of some of the problems posed. So that he may 'test' the group's capabilities, the director takes one of the problems brought up in this meeting. How will they deal with an old person found lying on the floor too weak to move: how will they make the person comfortable?

In groups of 4/5 the volunteers are asked to practise what they would do in such an emergency: the other groups will come and observe and see that the right amount of care is taken. Each group must be able to prove its concern and ability to deal with the situation.

The final problem that the meeting must tackle is posed by the director. It may be necessary at some time for members of the group to persuade an old person to move into a Home (an idea that had come up earlier but had been left). The director stresses that it is a very difficult subject to tackle: does anyone feel capable of so doing? Those who feel that they could must show the group how they will do this: the director will pretend to be the old man and the children must come and break the news, tactfully, to him. The rest of the group observe and learn. In pairs they practise with the partner how it could be done.

The teacher comes out of role and moves the group back to their original discussion area: they reflect on some of the problems raised by the subject matter of the lesson.

Strategies:

The use of role by the teacher (and therefore a formalised language).

A map drawn on the board — to give a location.

Group ideas listed on board for consideration.

Written work — to focus individual ideas.

The use of practice situations — one can always fail since it is just a practice — providing the situation is set up as seriously and with as much care as everything else.

Retelling the story and discussion to re-inforce achievement.

LESSON 14

OLD PEOPLE (2)

3rd year Juniors; 20 children; school hall

Lesson time: 40 minutes

Objective: A lesson using the same theme as in Lesson 13, and with the same objective.

The teacher is going to work with the class in making up a play about old people. The play is going to take place in an old people's home. (This is as much as the teacher has planned in advance apart from the fact that he knows his role will be that of warden and that the issues which evolve will, he hopes, be concerned with the problems of caring for others). Although the group is able to negotiate fairly responsibly with the teacher, the members of the group do not easily negotiate with each other: the teacher hopes that an issue involving responsibility for others may help to improve this.

The teacher, as warden, welcomes members of group as new staff for the Home. He understands that they have been sent to him as highly skilled and qualified in dealing with old people. He would like to hear of their experience in other homes or, perhaps, the ways in which they have dealt with elderly individuals living in their own homes. The group needs to work out verbally what the main problems are going to be. The warden lists these problems.

The group feels that one of the major problems is how to deal with people whose sight is bad or who are blind. The warden agrees that this is indeed one of the main areas of concern. He would like to be assured of the group's competence in dealing with such cases: would it be possible for him to see how the staff might cope? He needs to be certain of their skill and their caring.

The meeting ends with the group members choosing the particular work they will do in the Home. (They find their own space in the hall in which to go about this 'work', e.g. maintenance work, cooking, gardening, helping 'imaginary' people walk round the Home).

The lesson ends with a short meeting to discuss any problems that may have arisen during their first day's work.

Assessment

There was no sequel to this lesson though possible areas of follow-through might be concerned with the problems of individual patients and the problems of responsibility (if a patient had become ill, or died, could we be sure it was not through negligence — if so would we strive to keep that a secret from press enquiries — a lot of manipulation by the teacher if he wants that situation to be set up).

This lesson was on a fairly superficial level: the group were not confronted with a problem sufficiently important to engage them in a deeper level of thought or feeling.

Strategies:

Introductory discussion.

Teacher in authority role.

List-making — to focus ideas.

Trust exercise — to increase concern and deepen commitment.

The work of the Home — mimed physical activity.

Discussion in role.

Basically the *TEACHER IN ROLE* since the class can now cope with this way of working.

Initial discussion with teacher explaining what the play is to be about.

The major part of the early discussion will this time be done in role (as below).

Teacher explains that he will start the play as 'somebody else'. He moves group to his 'office' in another part of hall and sets up the first meeting.

These are the clues (and more) which the teacher must give now to build the background to the play.

LIST-MAKING to focus on points raised. (Done here by teacher on big sheet of paper).

The teacher here uses a *DRAMA GAME/EXERCISE* within the context of the lesson: a pair trust exercise of blind leading is used with 1 partner as person who can't see: 'let me see the care you take of them.' The warden instructs and praises.

The teacher can come out of role to set this up or he might continue to give instructions as warden.

This section consists of fairly basic individual mime used to increase belief and concern.

Final discussion set up as a meeting in warden's 'office'. The teacher then comes out of role to discuss what has happened during the course of the play.

LESSON 15

REHOUSING (1)

2nd year Remedial Secondary; 20 girls; classroom

Objective: To establish a way of working which is very different from the kind of drama they have been used to. To encourage identification with a fictitious situation which goes beyond their usual comic, cliché style. To introduce a learning area, which will be explored through this identification, and which may give opportunities for writing, reading, drawing and other activities:

The teacher introduces the class to the kind of drama she is offering, and gains their interest. Feeds in the idea that she will take part in the drama in role.

TEACHER IN ROLE.

The beginnings of commitment, as they identify themselves.

TEACHER AS NARRATOR.

Copies of a real letter prepared in advance might be preferable.

Commitment to new housing; group decision-making and negotiation.

Teacher challenges one group in role.

Teacher as narrator using story as reinforcement.

The teacher explains to the girls that in order to save time, today they will not plan the play in advance. They will need to pick up clues and signals as the drama progresses. The teacher demonstrates by approaching one girl:

' "Good morning, Mrs. Jones. How many pints would you like today?" Who was I?' 'The milkman.' The class are interested and intrigued, but a few girls are not yet prepared to commit themselves to active involvement.

At the suggestion of the teacher, the class divide themselves into small family groups. It is suggested that it is afternoon, and they are the adult female members of the family.

In role, the teacher enters as a lady from the council, and knocks on each door. She says she is checking on all the people living in the street, and lists the members of each family. At this stage, there are signs of 'acting', some of the girls reply in 'posh' accents, and there is giggling.

The teacher tells the class that each family will receive a letter from the council, to tell them that they are to be re-housed. They will be invited to a meeting in the Town Hall. As postman, the teacher delivers imaginary letters to each family. There is immediate discussion and interaction among the neighbours, and definite attitudes are adopted: 'I'm not moving from here' 'My mother can't leave the street where she has lived all her life.'

The meeting is called. The children move from the different parts of the room which have been their 'houses' to a circle of chairs. The teacher, as council official, welcomes them and explains the situation. The council's new road plans mean that their street will have to be pulled down. There is an outcry from the girls. The official explains that because they have been given such short notice, they are to be the subject of an experiment. They will all be re-housed together, and the council will try to make sure that they get the kind of housing they need. They are asked to go home and prepare a list of their ten priorities to be included in their new homes.

The girls return to their family groups, and make their lists. One family includes an elderly grandmother. The council official visits them, and suggests that the grandmother should be sent to an old people's home. Here, the commitment of the girls to their family group is remarkable. The problem of coping with an elderly person is confronted without any 'acting', and with complete involvement in the make-believe.

Two girls, who so far have remained on the outskirts, merely observing, now present themselves as a young married couple, expecting their first baby.

The list of priorities is collected, and the families are called to another meeting.

The council's proposals are put to the group. Some of the demands — e.g. central heating — will be included in the plans, but on others there will be compromise. A swimming-pool in each garden is obviously impossible, and with young children, might prove dangerous. But the new development may include a pool among its amenities. The families are pleased, on the whole, but are already beginning to consider the cost of such a scheme, in rent, rates and heating bills.

The meeting is brought to a close.

The teacher re-inforces what the class has achieved by telling them the story of what has just occurred — about a tightly-knit community who face the threat of losing their homes, and what happens to them.

Assessment

Both teacher and class felt a sense of achievement after this lesson, although no drama in depth had occurred. The girls became quite involved with their 'homes' and 'families', and were pleased that their ideas were sought, accepted and put in a meaningful framework. They worked with almost complete concentration for an hour.

Future activities might include: Planning amenities for the new estate; Looking at and designing house plans; Selecting furniture and equipment; Writing a letter to the council.

Future developments of the theme might be: The problems facing the newly housed; The breaking-up of a community; Tower-blocks and New Towns; Isolation; Vandalism.

Strategies:

Teacher in role.

Small family groups.

Letter — to move drama on.

List-making — to build commitment.

House and Estate plans on blackboard — visual focus.

Discussion in role.

Story-telling to re-inforce achievement.

LESSON 16

REHOUSING (2)

16—17 year olds in assessment centre; 8 girls; classroom

Lesson time: 10 am — 4 pm

Objective: To establish a way of working in a new kind of drama, and to encourage the group to work together, which was difficult in such highly charged and disturbing surroundings.

The teacher uses exactly the same opening of the lesson as that in Lesson 15, although the girls refuse to move from the chairs on which they are sitting, and do not 'play at houses' as the previous class did. The class proceeds in almost the same way, until the council meeting is called. There is one attempt to 'throw' the teacher, by a girl who behaves as if she is very pregnant, causing laughter from the others. The teacher accepts this as part of the set-up, quite seriously.

TEACHER IN ROLE

The teacher, in role as council official, explains that their street will have to be pulled down. There is immediate outcry, as before, but unlike the previous situation the teacher is unable to mollify the group by suggesting that they will be rehoused. There is real anger against the bureaucracy of the council, which is probably quite understandable in the light of the girls' own experience. The teacher realises that unless she changes tack, the group will polarise firmly against her, which is seldom a useful experience. She checks that no one is listening outside the meeting room, and then admits to the group that, in her real opinion, they are perfectly right to oppose the council's plans, and that she will assist them in their opposition, although it may mean the loss of her job if this is discovered. Immediately the group are once again on her side.

Change of direction — modification of role.

The group begin to plan what measures they can adopt against the council — petitions, publicity, sit-ins. At this point one girl announces that she does not agree — she wishes to move from the street as she does not like her neighbours. Once again, the group seems about to divide. But this dissension in fact provides a real area of exploration for the group. They begin to adopt much clearer attitudes to each other, whereas up to this point their characters have been merely labels.

Teacher out of role; group in role, from time to time, at the suggestion of the rest of the group. A valuable exploration and reflection period.

The next hour and a half are spent seated in a circle, examining through role-play the attitudes of the neighbours to each other, and finding out something of their background. It is discovered that Mrs. Clark, the 'posh' neighbour, has a son who is the father of the pregnant girl's child. The group see them meet, and their reactions to each other. Many facets of life in the street are examined in this way, with the rest of the group asking questions, suggesting scenes which could be looked at, and discussing the motivations and characters of the people involved. Side issues which arise include how best a family of six can be accommodated in a two-bedroomed house, and during this period several girls who have remained on the periphery become really involved.

Change of focus.

After lunch, the teacher feels that a new focus for the work is needed. A couple of new people have joined the group, and have to be absorbed into the work.

Drawing and writing to deepen commitment.

She returns to the idea of the rehousing, and asks the different family groups (three) to draw ground plans of their homes in detail. She asks one girl, a leader in the group, but potentially very disruptive, to act as the interviewer on a local radio programme which is to be made about the scheme.

Teacher changes role to a challenging, authoritarian role.

Using a cassette tape recorder, Marcia interviews the different families about their views on the council's plans. The teacher has prepared a large map of the proposed scheme, and its alternatives, and this is used as a basis for the discussion. After a time, the teacher joins in as a local councillor who wholly supports the council's scheme, and can act as a focus for the resentment of the group. At this point, there is no danger of alienating the group, since all are engaged in the same exploration.

When the radio discussion ends, the teacher suggests that several months have passed, and asks the class to accept that they have won their case, and are now firmly established in their homes. The council has agreed to give them help in improving their homes, and asks them to decide what changes they will make in their housing. While they are doing this, she asks Marcia, still choosing to be an outsider, to prepare a list of children who need to be fostered or adopted by secure and happy homes. Marcia does this with great skill, suggesting quite detailed and realistic case-histories for a number of children.

Teacher hands over control to a member of the class.

The families are brought together, and Marcia explains that their help is needed in caring for these children. Could they accept them into their homes? A deep and most interesting discussion ensues with the group absolutely in role, about the varying needs of the children, and their ability to help. Marcia, with the teacher as a second-in-command, asks to view their homes before making a decision about housing the children, and is shown carefully, and in great detail, round the ground plans of the houses, which have already been drawn. She reserves judgement, and promises to let the families know her decision.

A new stimulus is introduced, to deepen the work already achieved.

The lesson ends here, at four o'clock.

Assessment

The crucial factor in this lesson was the length of time available — a whole day. Concentration never wavered on the part of the group, in spite of the length of time for which they had been working. Because time was available, the teacher felt free to explore meaningful areas in considerable depth, and was not driven to finding some kind of instant satisfaction for the group. At the end, the group seemed to feel a real sense of achievement, and that they had been engaged in a significant exploration of real problems. Some of the situations explored paralleled their own difficult circumstances fairly closely, yet were sufficiently distanced by the drama to enable them to be examined objectively.

Strategies:

Teacher in role 1st — sympathetic official
2nd — authoritarian official

Exploration through role-play, in pairs and threes.

Map of road scheme — as visual focus.

House plans — as focus for ideas, and to deepen commitment.

Radio programme — to enable the group to discuss the issues in role.

Case histories — to provide information and a basis for work.

LESSON 17

TRANS-SIBERIAN EXPRESS

For any number of Secondary Pupils who have a secure relationship with the teacher. This lesson works well with a class where there are some aggressive (and dominating) individuals

Lesson time: 75 minutes

Objective: To use a highly structured and controlled form to enable a class to intensify a personal language experience.

A Quiet Start

Some members of class are told that there is a special task for them. They must wait. Everyone else is given a simple travel permit or passport form to fill up. They are travelling on a long journey across Northern Europe which has already taken days. It is winter. They are to assume an identity and reason for travelling from (let us say) China to Berlin or any other place in the Northern part of Europe. The class is warned that they will have to live with these characters and that it is unwise to choose anything too bizarre.

While this is being completed the others are called together and briefed. They will be guards and spy-catchers. The travellers are to be questioned in order to try and find a spy, who is rumoured to be on the train. They will have to be thorough and quick. Anyone whose story sounds false or whose behaviour is uncharacteristic should be suspect. They are to arrange their part of the room as interrogation areas.

Papers completed, passengers are asked to make themselves as comfortable as possible, as if sleeping on a train in cramped conditions. They may arrange chairs at the other end of the room from the guards.

Guards and interrogators are called together quietly and have a small conference and check on arrangements. The teacher says that he will adopt a supervisory role.

Guards go along 'train' and ask to see papers, they collect them and take them to interrogators who decide who to interview first. Guards marshal and control passengers.

The rest of the lesson develops as it will.

The 'passengers' may draw lots before filling up forms. The one with the X is the spy but no-one else knows. This then becomes a game or test of wits. Many classes are happier with this as a control. An experienced class may prefer that the passengers do not know why they are being stopped in the middle of the night.

The choice of the 'bossy' pupils as interrogators is a safe one. It may well be that the teacher wishes to reverse this for particular reasons.

Strategies:

Teacher in supervisory role.

Class divided into travellers and guards.

Travel-permits — to establish identity.

Arranging the 'train' — physical activity.

Interrogation — verbal commitment.

The teacher issues instructions.

'Form' invented or plain paper used and questions dictated.

A map may be useful.

Some background may be given here and a time-limit for completing the task.

The teacher tries to avoid the suggestion of brutality by concentrating on character-reading.

No mention of what will happen to them.

The teacher in role may question and even provoke, or subdue and support.

ASPECTS OF DRAMA

The following section deals, fairly briefly, with a number of different aspects of drama. It is by no means a comprehensive list of such aspects, nor can we, in the scope of this present document, hope to deal exhaustively with any one of these aspects. This particular list has been chosen in order to develop in more detail some of the strategies referred to in the first section and illustrated in the lesson examples.

Some of the ideas touched on in this section may provide a bridge for some teachers between the kind of drama they are engaged in at present, and the direction in which they hope to develop.

MOVEMENT

The kind of movement described in this section need not necessarily be used only as a limber at the beginning of a lesson, but can also be included within the context of a lesson where this is appropriate. Often, teachers wish to establish a change of mood at the start or finish of a drama lesson, and here the sections on Movement, Relaxation, and Games may be of use. But teachers should be aware of what kind of atmosphere they are trying to create, and whether these activities will further their aims in the drama.

The following movement activities are based on the work of Veronica Sherborne. They are in no way connected with any technicalities of dance, nor with quality of movement as may be aimed at in a dance/movement session, but are designed to get the children moving, involved in the lesson and relating to each other. All of Veronica Sherborne's exercises are very much 'experiences', and very real ones at that. Not only are they intensely physical, demanding strength, concentration and awareness, but because pupils are usually required to work in pairs or groups, they must learn to relate to and become aware of each other. Trust, sensitivity, and good group relationships can grow rapidly from the skilful use of these exercises. It should also be possible for the teacher to observe his class during these activities, and notice those children who find it difficult to trust themselves to others, those with a great sense of security, and those with little awareness of themselves or other people.

Strength

Working in pairs: (Referred to as A and B)

1. A to take up a firm position on the floor while B tries in various ways to move him.

2. A and B sitting back to back, pushing hard against one another — test partner's anchorage. Follow on from this for both partners to rise together with backs touching from base to neck.

3. A anchor to the floor using hands and feet — B try to hang on to A in various ways.

4. Same anchorage as for 3 but this time B to try and lift partner from the floor by grabbing under the arms, anchored member to try and escape.

5. A lie flat on the floor using spreadeagled hands and feet for anchorage while B sits on his back. A to try and get up. B try and prevent this.

6. Both partners pushing strong shoulder to shoulder (rugby scrum).

7. A standing with feet flat on the ground (wide base), knees slightly bent (this position gives sideways stability but is less stable backwards and forwards). B to use strength to try and move partner who is holding position.

8. Both A and B to take up firm stance with knees slightly bent and push against partner sideways — equal pressure from both students.

Support Relationships

Working in threes: (Referred to as A, B and C)

1. A and B support C by holding his arms and help him to jump. This is a good way to start a lesson, it helps to ease initial tension, builds confidence and helps inter-relation in groups.

N.B. In all these exercises it is important to ensure a wide firm base using feet and hands flat against the floor. Strength and stability together need a position close to the ground. For greatest stability the centre of gravity must be low.

When working in pairs allow A and B to change places and repeat experience.

2. A and B support C, who wriggles in as many ways as possible. Try for flexibility.

3. A and B support and control the movement of C by holding him firmly by the arms. C should anchor his feet, relaxing the top half of his body and allowing it to be manipulated by the supports.

4. C to lie on the floor with knees bent up. A and B support, lift his head off the floor and sway him gently from side to side with his head hanging loose.

5. Supports catch the weight of third member on their backs as he falls freely forwards and backwards. A should bend with the weight and then transfer to B. The quality of support is very important, the taking and giving of weight should be felt.

100% Support (Total commitment)

1. A and B kneel on all fours while C stretches across them, back to backs. Supports rock gently. Lower gently to the floor by moving slowly sideways and down while at the same time steadying C with one arm.

Groups of four or more:

1. Four students support and carry a fifth.

2. Four students hold a fifth by the arms and legs and swing him.

3. Any number of supports lie on the floor — one student stretch across the top of them, supports then move passenger along by rolling.

Support and Trust (50/50 Relationships)

1. Pairs sitting back to back, standing and sitting together, whole of spine touching.

2. A and B stand together back to back and travel sideways, then in different directions.

3. A and B rest against one another, back to back, heads relaxed.

4. Balance in pairs face to face. Firm stance with knees bent and feet apart to give stability. Both partners grip the other's wrists and keeping backs straight rise and lower.

5. Maintain 50/50 balance and spin.

6. A maintain balance alone with eyes closed while B walks round and selects a new partner. Take hands and balance with new partner. (Communication necessary in order that partners may relate to each other).

7. One of each pair holding elbows and helping partner to jump.

Free Flow Activities

Individual:

1. Sitting on the floor, spinning round and stamping feet.

2. Lying on the floor — spinning round on stomach — using hands to 'walk' round.

3. Lying on the floor — rolling in a relaxed position, arms above the head.

Pairs:

1. A to pull B along by holding his ankles.

2. A to pull B along getting a sway from the waist. (B must be completely relaxed).

3. Both students standing. A spin B round holding at the wrists. B drop to the floor and be spun in a sitting position held by one or two wrists.

4. A to lie on his side while B rocks him gently from side to side.

These exercises create excellent relationships within the group, especially if pupils are encouraged to change partners frequently.

It can be a good idea to begin a lesson with free flow movement as this will change a mood from one of inertia and create a feeling of elation. Too much prolonged free flow can have an intoxicating effect so variety must be given and bound or controlled flow introduced.

When working with handicapped or disturbed children, it is important to build a good rapport between teacher and pupil. Suggestion for this is that the teacher should make a 'chair' for the child by cradling him between the legs, the child's head relaxed and the teacher then gently rock him.

Many disturbed children will use free flow movement as a drug — they are desensitising themselves and preventing messages getting through to their brains. Continued free flow movement can send them to sleep.

Handicapped children do well on strength activities but they need time before fine touch can be achieved.

Fine Touch

Individual:

Lying on the floor, experiment with hands and fingers — float them in the air and around one another.

Pairs:

1. Watching partner's hands as they drift and float around in the air.

2. Both partners moving their hands at the same time, meeting and separating.

3. Both partners sitting on the floor facing — using hands lightly, picking up, flicking etc.

4. Begin with A sitting, B to raise him and guide him round the room using finger tip touch. Partner must respond to the messages received through touch.

In her article in 'Drama & Theatre in Education' Veronica Sherborne writes about her work with handicapped children, but it is generally applicable.

'Communication through movement is particularly necessary for them and I have noticed how much more normal children also benefit from using movement as a way of expressing themselves. There are two things here: one can use movement as a way of making contact with other people, and as a non-verbal way of expressing something about oneself.

In my work with mentally handicapped children I have noticed how the children have little or no sense of awareness of their bodies. When they are encouraged to become aware of their knees, feet, their hands, and perhaps of their bodies as a whole, they become more aware of themselves. They can be helped to develop a stronger sense of being a person, they can discover some sense of identity. I have observed this developing self-awareness in normal children, in students, in teachers, and in actors, and part of my programme is to work on strengthening self-awareness through increasing bodily awareness.'

RELAXATION

Often a class arrives for drama in an excitable and noisy state and before any sensitive and concentrated work can begin a short time spent in calming the children may be very necessary. Sometimes a vigorous physical warm-up may calm very excited children, by using up some of their excess energy and, for this purpose, many of the Veronica Sherborne exercises in the Movement Section can be employed. Often a more relaxing atmosphere is needed and one of the following exercises may prove useful. Such exercises may also serve to 'bring down' a class whose work has been very intensive and emotional and who need to be passed on to their next class in a more placid frame of mind.

Some of the games and exercises in Guidelines may well serve this purpose as may lying and listening to a piece of music or being 'talked through' a peaceful scene such as being on a beach, wading through water or one of the following:

Exercise One

Working individually — imagine that you are a candle. It burns down very slowly, and at last goes out. Alternatively, be a snowman melting in hot sun.

Exercise Two

Find a spot around the edge of the room. It is a small spot of shade in the desert. After a few moments you imagine you can hear a rustling sound. Can it be rain? Feel the drops cool on your tongue, face, hands, back of your neck. It is really raining quite hard. Try to shake the water off your hands, throw your arms loosely to get rid of the wet. Shake feet and legs loose. Shake all over like a wet animal does. (Lips and cheeks blown loose in the kind of shuddering noise that seems appropriate for such a movement is both fun and relaxing).

Exercise Three

Lying in a space on the floor. Relaxing and tensing — Imagine that you are lying, fast asleep, on your back, hands loosely by your side, feet falling slightly apart from the ankles. While you are sound asleep some devious villain creeps in and without waking you fastens your ankles and wrists down very firmly. Try to burst out of the bonds that hold you.

These exercises (3 & 4) also use a considerable amount of energy, but since the class are working individually they should not lead to any increase in the excitement level of the class.

Exercise Four

Allowing plenty of space between you and your neighbours, make yourself as small as possible on the floor. Imagine you are on a deserted shore and that you have been shut up inside a plastic bubble (or genii's bottle) for a thousand years. Try to kick, tear or bite your way out. There's no room to stretch out. When you burst out, try to imagine what it is like to have to learn to move again after so long.

GAMES

When faced with a new class, many teachers decide to use games as a starting point or 'way in' to drama and such a decision is certainly valid, since many games provide secure frameworks within which communication can easily be established. They are also a means of releasing tension, giving enjoyment, establishing relationships and increasing the group's level of self-control. That groups are capable of accepting the 'contract' of new rules for different games and realise that success and maximum enjoyment depend on the group's willingness to play the game, can be considered valuable preparation for drama in which the flexibility to adjust to new rules and situations is vital.

The playing of games is usually overwhelmingly successful and entertaining, and it is often difficult for both teacher and class to see such activity as only a beginning or initial stimulus to the actual work in a lesson. This is understandable especially when faced with difficult groups who insist on repeating games each lesson and refusing different approaches to work — games then become synonymous with drama and new teaching and control problems result.

There is no easy answer to this problem except to suggest that games, as with all good things, should be used in moderation, that they should not become part of the lesson routine and that their greatest value is only realised if they are used to develop and extend the learning area which both teacher and group have agreed to explore together.

A SELECTION OF GAMES

Introducing

For these 4 games, players sit in a circle.

1. A stands, introduces himself to C, etc. quickly, until all are standing.

2. A introduces himself. 'I am Paul.' B says, 'This is Paul, I am Sheila.' C says, 'This is Sheila, I am David,' etc. all round.

3. A says, 'I am Paul.' B says, 'Paul, Sheila.' C says, 'Paul, Sheila, David.' Each player names those before him, and adds his own name.

4. First player ascertains names of players to his right and left. All others find name of player on left. Then, going in clockwise direction, each player introduces righthand neighbour and lefthand neighbour.

Mixing

1. Players sit in circle on chairs, one player in middle. Player in middle asks one in circle, 'Do you like your neighbours?' If the answer is, 'Yes, very much' the two players either side of the speaker change places. If the answer is, 'No, not at all' everyone changes places. Either way, player in middle tries to sit in a chair, and the one left without a chair goes into the middle.

2. Players sit in circle on chairs, one player in middle. Player in middle names players in circle alternately ORANGE or GRAPEFRUIT. If he then calls ORANGES all the Oranges change places, if he calls GRAPEFRUIT all the Grapefruits change places, If he calls FRUIT BOWL all the players change places. Player in middle tries to sit in a chair, and one without a chair goes to the middle.

These games tend to become extremely noisy, and will probably produce a high state of excitement in the group.

Concentration and Co-ordination

1. The 'accumulation' game — of which there are many versions, e.g. A says 'I like apples,' B says 'I like apples and beetroots,' C says 'I like apples, beetroots and caviar,' and so on, each player adding another food beginning with another letter of the alphabet.

2. Mimed Objects. The class sit in a circle. One person picks up an imaginary object — e.g. a comb, a lollipop — and after using it for a moment to allow the rest of the group to identify it, he passes it to the next person, who also uses it. Then he reshapes it into another object, uses that, and passes it on.

A very quiet game. Useful for concentration and for developing the ability of the group to work with imaginary objects, which can be very important in drama.

3. Simon Says (or The Witch says, the Boss says). Mime action and fairly complicated movement can be introduced, appropriate to the kind of character who is leading the group.

4. Follow the Leader. Different people take turns as leader, and the leadership changes smoothly, without any pause in the actions.

All these games are valuable for getting the whole group working together, and giving different children the opportunity to lead the rest of the class.

5. Guess the leader. A goes out of the room. The others form a circle and pick a leader. A returns to the middle of the circle. The leader begins a simple action, very slowly, which the rest of the group follow, changing the action when A isn't looking. A tries to detect the leader.

6. Winking Murder. Organised as in the game above, but now the leader kills people by winking at them when A is not looking. A tries to detect the killer. Deaths can be spectacular.

Game Sample Lesson

Hunter and Hunted

This game is excellent for developing group control and considerable involvement.

1.   The group should all be sitting on chairs/stools or standing in a large circle. The larger the diameter of the circle, the better for the success of the game.

If a strong sense of ritual is gradually built into this game, it can be a most successful way of co-ordinating a class. Useful too if the teacher joins in.

2.   Two people, perhaps the quietest, are chosen. One is the hunter and the other the hunted. They must, when told, shut their eyes and keep them shut until the action is completed. Or they can be blindfolded.

Encourage 'handlers' to be gentle with blindfolded people. Each in turns discovers how frightening it can be not to use sight.

3.   Two other people take charge of the two players. The players' eyes shut, and the players are led to another part of the circle and gently turned round three times. The assistants sit down.

4.   When they are completely still, the teacher says, 'The game has started.' The two protagonists then start to move. The hunter must try to listen for the whereabouts of the hunted and catch the victim. The rest of the group must try to protect the protagonists from bumping into objects or moving through any gaps which might be in the circle.

Approach to Moliere's 'The Imaginary Invalid' (starting with the game 'Boring Your Partner')

This academic shy class had never done drama before and were about to study Moliere's 'The Imaginary Invalid' in French.

Started with a game, lasting one minute, which got them talking with no pressure, since everyone was talking simultaneously.

1.   The children worked in pairs, sitting at their desks. At a given signal each looked her partner in the eye and tried to talk, without pause, till stopped.

Development into dialogue, however successful or unsuccessful, involves listening but with competitive pressure to get in and speak. Dominant topics began to emerge. Continued until everyone seemed to have got into their conversation.

2.   Development of same game; this time they talked to each other one at a time, jumping into any pause, using any association of ideas to interrupt and dominate the conversation.

Introduction of relevant topic after preliminary work. Introduction of simple role-play, without their being aware of this step.

3.   Repeat of 1 and 2 on the topic of one's health.

Still in 'game' framework, still at desks, but gaining practice at improvising speech.

4.   Development of the same game into groups of about 8 in one conversation, each trying to monopolise on the subject of her own health.

Discussion based on their work, having 'cheated' them into role-playing hypo-chondriacs. (If you behave in a certain way you can be said to have played the role of someone who by definition behaves in that way!) Discussion continued until all the three possible attitudes to hypochondria used in 6 had been mentioned.

5.   Discussion of hypochondriacs and how they are treated.

More complex work but preceded by preparatory stages. Larger groups, but no splitting or rearranging of partners. Individualised roles. Dramatic situation follows Moliere: A = the imaginary invalid, B = the maid, C = the doctor, D = the brother. Continued till everyone had tried several roles.

6.   Pairs joined up to make 4's (with extra 2 or 3's). Desks adjusted where necessary. A, B, C, D. A is hypochondriac, B scornful of her, C humours her, D tries to get her to be different. Turn the roles till most have had a go at all 4 roles.

No pressure to show, but for those who chose to do so, an experience of presentation. Discussion of the relevance of the work to 'The Imaginary Invalid'.

7.   Some groups showed their work to the rest of the class.

The next lesson developed towards simple improvisation of situations in the play.

The Reporting Game

A game *developing from* improvisation instead of *leading into* it. Organisation difficult as some children had to be outside the room for some of the time. In practice the teacher had two improvisations and games operating in one session, but this is the basic outline.

1. A group prepared in secret a short realistic scene: 'An unusual incident in an everyday environment.' (e.g. theft of a statue from a museum.)

The example given here was particularly apt as it was capable of misinterpretation; the statue looked like a body.

2. 6 children sent outside — 3 'reporters' and 3 'sub-editors'.

Group informed rest of class of the time and place (e.g. midnight, outside the Louvre) and performed their scene. 3 of the onlookers were 'eye-witnesses' who moved freely, independently and silently through the scene, with their hands cupped to make a telescope over one eye, and the other shut, thus with restricted vision of the incident. Rest of class watched from around the playing area.

3. The 3 reporters from outside came in and were placed along one side of the room. The 3 eye-witnesses along the opposite side, each facing a reporter. Rest of class in the space between. Each eye-witness 'phoned' through his account of the incident to the reporter facing him, hindered by the rest of the class who created 'interference on the line'. One minute allowed.

Time allowed was decided after seeing the scene and considering the 'interference' the class was likely to make!

4. Without any pause or opportunity for consultation by the reporters, the 3 sub-editors were brought in from outside. The 3 reporters each had 30 seconds to tell one of the sub-editors his version of what occurred.

Time decided after previous stage.

Again, timing as appropriate.

5. The sub-editors had 1½ minutes to write as sensible an account as they could, without further consultation with anyone, including each other.

6. Class listened to the accounts read out. Compared all three versions, then compared all stages. Discussion on distortion of information..

Good introduction to work on mass media reporting.

PREPARED IMPROVISATION

'Divide into your groups. You have twenty minutes to prepare an improvisation on Aggression.'

For many teachers, the above represents a basic strategy. The theme may be chosen after consultation with the group, and discussion of the implications of that theme may have taken place, but the bulk of the lesson will be spent in preparing and showing a small group improvisation. If this structure is to be used, it is vital that teachers should understand what they may hope to achieve from working in this way.

In prepared improvisation, the group is working towards a finished dramatic statement — they are making up a play, in effect. A statement implies communication, even if the audience is only the teacher or the rest of the class. During the process of improvisation, ideas are refined and shaped, problems are solved, choices are made, and a dramatic form is sought which will express those ideas. The need to communicate requires the group to organise their ideas into a structure which will be communicable to others. Important learning areas can be opened up through this kind of work. It may assist pupils to understand and develop narrative structure, to select and shape their ideas, to develop language suitable to the subject, to express themselves coherently, to share decisions with the rest of the group.

However, since they are working in improvised play-making, technical considerations will also be important. Speech must be audible, and action must be effective. The need for technical skills of presentation will increase as the kind of audience becomes larger and more formal. To share ideas developed during the drama lesson with others as, for example, at assembly or parents' evening, will require further emphasis on theatrical skills. Perhaps this is the most difficult drama structure to operate effectively.

The difficulties inherent in this kind of structure are many. Too often, the group statements may degenerate into clichéd situations and stereotyped characterisations. The satisfaction to be enjoyed from the reception of their efforts by the rest of the group may encourage 'showing-off', and an over-indulgence in comic and caricatured performances. Frequently, the group may rely on one or two people to do the planning. Groups may become close-knit, and refuse opportunities to work with other than the same few friends. Because this method is wasteful of time, real reflection on what has been offered may be impossible.

If pupils become accustomed to working in this way, and the teacher is dissatisfied with the quality of their work, it may be very difficult for him to intervene effectively. The class may be divided into as many as half-a-dozen groups, and the problems for the teacher are therefore multiplied. For the inexperienced teacher, or one who has problems of control, this can be very unsatisfactory. Too often, his function may be merely giving the initial stimulus, and orchestrating the final 'showing' of the results. It may be almost impossible for the teacher to affect what is happening in the groups, to challenge the pupils, or to make the work more thoughtful. Many teachers are, in any case, unwilling to intervene, seeing this as interference with the pupils' creativity. Yet, left to themselves, pupils are unlikely to make real discoveries or extend themselves in the work.

If this kind of structure is felt to be the best way of working, or appropriate to the needs of the group, or is the only way in which the group are prepared to work, then the teacher must somehow find a way of challenging the group and not merely allow them to reiterate what they already know. The aim should always be towards quality, not merely of presentation skills, but of the ability to examine the implications of the material on which they are working, and of their ability to communicate their findings effectively to others.

With a group or a teacher who finds real security in this way of working, there are ways to make the small-group experience feed directly back to the whole group, so that it can become a focus for the work of the class.

In this example, the teacher divided the class into groups of five or six. Each group prepared and showed an incident in which one of the group was faced with a problem — either financial, social or personal. When all of the groups had shown their scenes, the teacher chose one — not necessarily the best acted — but the one which provided the rest of the group with the possibility of further inquiry, because of its implications.

The scene chosen was one in which a woman visits the welfare office to demand the return of her children who have been taken into care. The scene included two welfare officers, the woman, her mother, a neighbour, and a policewoman who was summoned to the scene. These pupils retained their roles, and the rest of the class was organised as follows:

Reporters from a local newspaper, writing up the incident.

Reporters from a national newspaper — either quality or tabloid.

Reporters from a local radio station, preparing a short item about the incident, using a cassette tape recorder.

The group whose scene it was were interviewed, and also had tasks of their own to complete — the welfare officials and policewoman writing reports for their superiors, and the others preparing their story for the newspapers.

By the time these tasks were completed, and the class had heard the results, there was a great deal of information available as to the background to the incident, and the possibility of further improvisation on the same theme, but at a more committed level.

Another example of the same structure is where the original incident is set on board a ship filled with immigrants to America during the 1890's. A single incident is once more chosen and the tasks set are as follows:

A newspaper report.

An historian's account of the incident.

A welfare organisation's report on conditions aboard.

A report containing advice to intending immigrants.

An anti-immigration report, using the incident in a biased way, for a newspaper.

Letters home to Europe from those on board.

Entries in the diaries of the immigrants.

Recollections of the event from years later.

Without using written tasks, there are many ways in which small-group play-making can still be a purposeful tool in the hands of the teacher. In the first example, instead of writing, the other groups could have formed themselves into agencies to help the family in various ways. Interviews and discussion would still be necessary, to establish background and a more thorough understanding of the problem, and the various groups could either report on their findings and their solution to the problem or actually show the solution of the problem by improvising the scene in which it happens. Other possibilities might be for the various groups to improvise and show scenes either earlier or later in the life of the family which figured in the original incident. In the second example of the immigrants, this approach could also be used — to show the pressures which led the people to emigrate in the first place, and something of their history after they arrived in America.

Small group play-making may be one of the most difficult drama structures to operate effectively, but with careful planning by the teacher, and sensitive direction of the pupils' attention, observation and reflection, this kind of structure can feed the experience of the whole class.

SPONTANEOUS IMPROVISATION

In spontaneous improvisation, whether initiated by the teacher or by the pupils, the quality of response will be very different from that in prepared improvisation, even where preparation time is limited to a matter of minutes. Since the experience is happening *then*, for the group, and it is the process which is important, there is no need to repeat it for others, nor would it be appropriate to do so. The pupils are faced with the need to respond immediately within the fictional situation. They are challenged by what takes place; they have to find clues and directions within the work; they have to negotiate directly with the teacher and the rest of the group; they have to find language appropriate to the situation. If the commitment to the drama is sufficiently strong, language will arise out of a real need to speak.

In this kind of approach, the teacher does not look for any technical skills of presentation or characterisation, but for what happens within the drama, and the qualities of thinking and feeling which are revealed. It will soon become apparent which children are able to accept the make-believe, to initiate ideas for the group, to respond to and build on the ideas of others.

It is possible for the class to develop spontaneous improvisation without the teacher acting as initiator, if he feels that it may be inappropriate for him to take part in the drama. If he remains on the outside of what is happening, he may be able to observe what is happening very closely, and the response of his class within the situation, although he will be unable to affect what is happening.

The following examples are of a teacher helping his class to begin this kind of work, and training them in some understanding of the 'rules of the game'. Other examples are given at the beginning of several of the lesson examples in the previous section.

The class sit in a circle. The teacher emphasises that the play takes place *only* in the circle. He gives an example of going into a shop to buy some cigarettes — leaving the circle to do so. He then gives them the correct example, within the circle.

Next, he gives a line to the class as he walks into the circle — 'One pint for me, please, Mabel. What are you having, George?' Then by questioning the class he finds out what signals they have picked up.

Then he walks into the circle holding his jaw. 'I haven't got an appointment, but can you fit me in?' Again, he checks the signals they have received.

This time he walks into the circle and mimes lighting a cigarette, and stands waiting. Nothing happens. He leaves the circle before asking them 'Are you going to let me stand there all day?' He returns to the circle and repeats the action, and this time one of the class joins him in a bus queue.

While they are getting used to the method, they can only contribute if they are in the circle — the only place where the play exists — and which acts as a physical focus for what is happening.

After a time, the pupils can themselves initiate the action, and become increasingly subtle and complex in their selection of signals and starting points for the rest of the class. The teacher should avoid, however, turning this into another exercise or guessing-game. The aim should be to build on what is offered, so that it becomes significant, and this may be very difficult to achieve while the teacher remains outside the drama.

ROLE~PLAY

Role-play exercises make some of the same demands as spontaneous improvisation, although the role may have been much more fully structured by the teacher. In role-play exercises, as in drama, the participants project themselves into a fictitious situation, and assume attitudes which are not necessarily their own, and which may in fact be the reverse of their real attitudes. These attitudes are usually imposed or suggested by the teacher, rather than the children discovering their attitudes from within the dramatic situation. No characterisation in the theatrical sense, or acting, is required, although characterisation may grow as the participants move from a generalised approach to a grasp of specifics. Since the participants are required to present attitudes with some realism, they will become aware of the demands of the role in real life. Each role requires the pupils to adopt a different relationship with other people, a different status, appropriate use of language, and varying behaviour expectations.

Of the many strategies used in drama teaching, role-play is perhaps the most easily accessible to teachers of other disciplines. It can be used briefly to illustrate a particular teaching point, or developed to examine a number of issues. It makes no excessive demands on the skill of the teacher, and can be operated in any normal classroom. But as in every drama lesson, the teacher using role-play needs to be clearly aware of his aim in setting up a particular exercise or situation. It can be invaluable in the following ways:

To achieve understanding of particular feelings, or points of view.

To clarify and crystallise an issue.

To establish particular facts.

To examine language, or status.

To illuminate a text.

As far as the drama teacher is concerned, role-play exercises, although perhaps limiting at first, can help to establish the following important areas for his pupils:

Help them to gain confidence, in a reasonably secure situation.

Show them that their ideas will be accepted and used.

Allow them to gain practice in adopting different attitudes.

Give them practice in using varying levels of language.

Give them practice in negotiating with other people.

Give them practice in problem-solving, decision-making and situation resolving.

Show them that thoughtful examination of the activity will follow.

Establish that 'showing the work' is not necessary.

Give them practice in coping with new situations.

Exercises in role-play can be structured in many different ways, as in the following examples:

Pairs:

Two friends — A and B. B tells A what he did during last weekend.

A is now B's parent. B tells A what he did last weekend. Has his story altered?

A is a policeman and is questioning B. He does not tell B what he is suspected of doing, but asks him to dictate a statement about his movements last weekend. Then he cross-questions B about his statement, and tries to incriminate him. How does B react?

A and B. A is the new manager of a factory, and has to tell B, an old and valued employee, that he is about to be made redundant.

In threes:

The teacher briefs each one separately as to their role.

A, B and C are friends. A has lost a £5 note and accuses B of taking it. In fact, C is guilty. How does C react?

A, B and C are friends. A and B want to go to a party, which will involve staying out late at night. They want C to pretend to their parents that they are both staying the night at C's house. Does C agree?

In larger groups:

The pupils are residents on a housing estate. A meeting has been called to try to deal with vandalism which is rife. What decisions are taken?

The class, as parents, are called to a meeting at the school which their children attend. There have been reports of indiscipline and falling standards in the local paper. How can they help the teachers to alter this?

In role-play, no dramatic statements are being formulated, so showing will not be appropriate. The class may pause to observe some of its members working in role at times, perhaps in order to illustrate particular points which the teacher wishes them to notice about the work, but since they are all engaged in the same exploration, they are never merely passive spectators.

The teacher may find that the first attempts of his class at role-play seldom go beyond cliché and stereotype. Without rejecting these, he must find the means of extending his pupils' understanding, and moving them on from these stock responses. Useful ways of achieving this may be to alter the situation or inject some kind of role-reversal or challenge to their thinking, e.g. an irresponsible parent, or a dishonest judge, or he may be able to move them on by entering the situation in role himself.

Again, as in all other drama lessons, the reflective phase of a lesson spent in role-play exercises will be vital. The pupils will not deepen their understanding of human behaviour merely by adopting roles, but will need to reflect on the experience with the help of the teacher's questioning.

Role-play exercises can lead on to the kind of drama where roles are no longer imposed externally, and where pupils develop real commitment to the activity. As a preparation for this kind of drama, teachers who wish to work in role themselves with their classes, may find that through role-play exercises they can readily accustom their pupils to accepting them in a variety of roles.

TEACHER IN ROLE

A large proportion of the lessons in this edition of Drama Guidelines illustrate the concept of the teacher working in role. In this way he will engage in the progress of the drama alongside his pupils and can thereby more effectively support their contributions, challenge their thinking, move the drama on, and, most important, by standing in the way of glib and facile solutions, slow down a drama that may be moving too fast. By adopting a role he may control, guide and shape the lesson from the inside: it can be an extremely economical way of working.

For many teachers however, the use of role may not be an easy, or immediately successful tactic. To a class unused to this method of working, the appearance of their teacher 'pretending' to be somebody else may be too funny or too embarrassing to have anything but an initially destructive effect, and the teacher, fighting to maintain an already shaky confidence, may all too readily abandon the attempt and not wish to repeat it. We hope that the following points may prove helpful to those teachers interested in the idea of using role.

Its usage does not require great acting skill, since what it implies is not so much the creation of a fully-rounded character as the adoption of a set of attitudes, the taking of a stance. What is needed above all, is seriousness and commitment to the role. The teacher who is unprepared or unable to bring to it these qualities is not likely to achieve much success in its use. A class may often greet a first attempt with giggles, but these will go if the teacher perseveres, since such a reaction is likely to be a form of defence against the strangeness of this new method, or, perhaps, a test of the teacher's commitment to it. If he is to ultimately ask for the belief and involvement of the children, he must first be prepared to give his. The teacher may be demanding that the children take a considerable initial risk in offering a response, since they will have to pick up signals from him without any time for planning ahead. They will need to gauge the measure of trust they may place in him before making a full commitment themselves. They will be testing the teacher before going along with him and he must give some guarantee that the smallest contribution will be heard and given support — it may have cost its contributor a great deal. It is important, for example, to encourage the timid child who, quite seriously, offers a model aeroplane as a gift for a primitive chieftain: the gift he makes must be accepted and made useful. A solemn nod may be enough recognition of its worth but if it can be made more significant then so much the better: 'It is the shape of the great eagle which guards our tribe. It will serve as a mascot for us.' Factual inconsistencies can be dealt with later. It is important for the progress of the drama lesson that such offerings are not dismissed as inaccurate or irrelevant, and they must be accepted in a serious and supportive way. The deliberately facile response is usually easily recognisable and can be tactfully ignored, challenged and put to some use, or, once gain, greeted with a solemn nod. Though other children may laugh at the funny and anachronistic remark, the teacher must not. A glib and self-mocking attitude in the teacher is in fact likely to produce the same kind of response in his class and this will effectively destroy the hope of achieving work of any depth.

If the teacher is about to work in role for the first time, it is wise to explain to the class what this method will involve, e.g. 'I shall be taking a part in the play with you.' It is useful to try out some short examples of this approach, and to give a very clear indication of the rules of this particular game: a chair might serve as a focus, a 'gathering around' area for when the teacher needs to momentarily halt the progress of the lesson — 'Whenever I come to sit on this chair I shall want you to stop what you are doing. It means that I shall want to talk to you again as teacher.' Once that rule is made it should be adhered to.

A great deal will, of course, depend on the way in which each lesson is set up. Beginnings should be clear and strong and direct. Though the eventual outcome of the lesson may depend on how the teacher shapes the pupils' contributions within the developing situation, the beginning of that lesson is the responsibility of the teacher alone and should therefore be carefully planned. He may explain the method of working and the rules of that method. He may introduce the theme of the lesson and provide some initial information to support the theme — all this needs to be explained clearly and simply. The bridge between class in discussion with teacher and the start of the play needs also to be stated with clarity: the following example might serve —

'I think we're ready to start the play now. I'm going to leave the group for a few moments and just go to the other end of the room. When I come back I shall speak to you as if I were somebody else and the play will begin.'

From this point on the teacher can stay in role until he needs to draw the group members together to discuss with them, as teacher, the progress of the lesson so far, the information that the development of the play has given them, and the possible directions that the lesson might now take since many options may now be revealed and the group will need to choose one of these before any further progression can take place. The discussion can be centred around the 'teacher chair' agreed on at the beginning of the lesson.

Though there may be some initial discussion of the lesson theme, and an initial input of information by the teacher, these should be as economical as possible. It is not helpful for the teacher to issue an over-long list of instructions or weigh down the children with a mass of information — the latter is often better done through role once the play has started:

'Now listen carefully please. We shall be leaving port soon. I am the officer in charge of this part of the ship. You will be spending the next eight days in this space until we arrive at New York. Keep your luggage with you and start making yourselves as comfortable as you can.'

These statements, offered in role, might be used to begin a lesson on immigration to the United States in the nineteenth century. The class through its responses and by its questioning, will ask for whatever else it needs to know as the lesson develops and the ability to provide this quickly and effectively is the responsibility of the teacher. The experience of the drama lesson may later lead into other areas of research: it is not necessary to have an encyclopaedic knowledge of the theme in advance. A great deal will depend on the ability to think quickly on one's feet and this is often an acquired skill.

Most children seem to find little difficulty in having their teacher move in and out of role, providing that this is done with clarity. Indeed, it is possible that the teacher may need to adopt more than one role in the course of the lesson, and, here again, the role needs to be introduced in such a way that the class is left in no doubt as to what the new role is.

The introduction of a second role may come from from the need to move the direction of the lesson into another area of exploration and so the initial role may seem less apropriate e.g., a class of immigrants, now arriving at New York might be met not by teacher as ship's officer but as customs official. The adoption of this role might be done following a mid-lesson discussion:

'When we start the play again, I shall become a different person from the one I have been up until now. This time I shall be someone inspecting the new arrivals in New York.'

The choice of the role open to the teacher is of course very wide and varied and will depend greatly on what the teacher wants his role to do. A most effective kind is that which allows the teacher to initiate a situation but which then permits him to step back from the centre of the action leaving this to the children. The messenger who brings news and then departs, the stranger who comes looking for shelter and does not know the ways of the tribe, and the apprentice who is new to his job — though these roles differ subtly one from another, they are of the kind which hands over a great deal of responsibility to the class. For this reason they can be very worrying to teacher security, so those teachers unused to this method may often find it easier to adopt an authority role through which control may, for the most part, stay firmly within their grasp. The chief, the King, the expert, the gang boss, the warden, the father, the captain, the wagon master, etc.: — these reflect a situation in which the teacher remains in charge, not far removed, indeed, from his normal role of teacher, and the class may have little difficulty in accepting this.

Whatever the role it will gain in strength from the teacher's selectivity of language. A more formal mode of speech will help greatly in that building of belief which is so important: it serves to make a distinction between the teacher as teacher and the teacher as, say, a knight. Language of this more elevated nature can add a tension and a concern to the drama and children find little difficulty in absorbing it.

'Let each man now state the purpose of his quest' —

is likely to contribute more to the belief of the class in its collective role as a knightly brotherhood than the more workaday —

'Now I want you to tell me what you're going to look for.'

The use of role can prove to be an enormously effective strategy but it is by no means an easy one to adopt and there may be times when the condition of a particular lesson indicates that it is going to be of greater value for the teacher to come out of role and pursue a different approach. Nothing is lost in doing this: far better to clearly and positively draw this approach to a close, than to pursue it against hopeless odds. The use of role may not always be appropriate and this can depend on such factors as the teacher's aims for the lesson, and the mood in which he and the class come to it. A teacher working in role, and finding himself frustrated by the inability of the children to offer him imaginary objects as gifts, may in fact gain more by coming out of role and setting up an exercise in which the class learns how to accept and handle such objects. There may also be times when it is better to turn a disintegrating lesson into a group discussion which may provide a valuable reflection on the lesson and the issues arising from it. The teacher may return to the use of role at another time when he feels the circumstances to be right and where his aims for the lesson are best fulfilled by using this particular method.

Summary

1. A teacher working in role for the first time will need to explain this method to his class. Some practice might be useful since the children will need to work quickly and pick up the signals the teacher offers. There is no advance planning since this will be a spontaneous activity.

2. Role should be used as and when the class is ready for it. The rules and conventions should be clearly explained at the beginning of each lesson until the group becomes familiar with them. These might include:

— the teacher takes a part in the play

— the group works together and everyone has a part

— the teacher may need to stop the play and draw the group to a discussion around a certain chair/area

— the play starts when the teacher enters in role.

These examples serve only as an illustration of how the lesson might be introduced: it may, for example, start with an activity (a village at work?) where the teacher gradually involves himself in role.

3. The use of role is a very economical and effective way of conveying information and reduces to a minimum the need for a long, explanatory introduction though the teacher may feel this helpful for building trust and confidence, etc.

4. The teacher in role must work seriously and convey this seriousness to the class. He must encourage their commitment by displaying his. He must let them know that they can trust him and be prepared to accept all contributions, bolstering those which need support, leaving aside those which may be irrelevant to the development of the theme, acting on those which open up fruitful areas of exploration. The teacher may need to adopt more than one role in the course of the lesson.

5. The choice of role is enormous but the teacher should decide what it is he wants the role to do. He may want to use it to guide, to advise, to threaten, to dispute, to be taught, etc. He should use role as and when appropriate.

6. Language, if used selectively by the teacher, is a great support to the authenticity of the role: it helps to build belief in it.

SOME WAYS IN

This edition of Drama Guidelines does not set out to provide a separate list of 'beginnings' though a number of examples may be found in the lesson plans and in those topics covered in Section 3. The following ideas, however, may serve as an indication of different approaches to one theme. In several cases they outline work that might be covered before the teacher uses drama to explore the theme in any depth, and will most probably reflect the kind of activity already being followed by many teachers. They are almost all classroom-based activities, and require little extra space. The examples listed formed part of a long-term integrated curriculum project on the Great Fire of London.

Building Family/Work backgrounds

The class works in small groups, using any information they have about 17th Century London. The group members decide on their individual activities as members of a family, or as members of a craft/guild group. Each group prepares a list of its members, giving details of age, address, occupation, etc., and these can form part of a census listing the whole class. This might form the basis for group reports on their work and background and for questioning or interviewing by the teacher and the other members of the class: the group members respond as the roles they have created. This can be a useful device for building a detailed background which will be of benefit in any subsequent drama work.

Working from a Photograph

A similar approach is one in which the teacher gives each group a photograph to work from — in this instance it may be of a contemporary fire incident. The group members are each asked to identify with one of the people in the photograph, and to prepare a 'biography' for that person. This can then lead to the same kind of interviewing and reporting as outlined above.

Improvisation/Teacher in Role

The teacher sets up a situation for the class and conveys information through his role e.g. he may be the leader of a group of citizens meeting in safety at Greenwich to consider whether they will return to the city. The teacher's aim is to focus the improvisation on specific aspects of the theme. The purpose is not to re-enact the known story, but to find areas of learning within it (e.g. do we, as citizens, have any evidence as to how the Fire started?: do we hold anyone responsible for its outbreak?: are we responsible for each other's safety and for the safety of those still in London?: what course of action do we now follow?) At the end of the improvisation it can often prove useful to list, on a board, the facts which have arisen from it: this draws together what we already know and can suggest possible areas of future development. The teacher will not need to impart a great deal of information before he begins the lesson. What the class knows about the subject — *and what it does not know* — will be made clear as the lesson progresses.

Working from a Map

The teacher uses a map to chart the (imaginary) progress of the Fire, and the extent of the destruction. This might be done with the teacher working in role (as mayor?) consulting with the class (as aldermen?) — focussing on such questions as: Can the Fire be checked? What arrangements are in hand for evacuation? This exercise helps, again, to build a more detailed background for further work, whether in drama or of another kind. As a conclusion to this theme the teacher may well use a similar strategy, e.g. Since much of the city has been destroyed, how shall we re-plan it? How can we improve on what was there before?

Reporting on an incident

Groups work on an incident from the Fire, and show this to the rest of the class. The teacher chooses one of these incidents — not necessarily the best acted, for that is not what is of importance here, but one which provides material in terms of 'newsworthiness'. The rest of the class will have been asked to observe each incident carefully and they are now asked to work as reporters, diarists, etc., interview the people involved in the incident, and prepare written accounts of what they have witnessed. These are then read back by them to the rest of the class. Some careful organisation is required here, so that everyone has a task, e.g. some may draw pictures to accompany the written accounts, members of the group involved in the incident may prepare their own diaries when not being interviewed, and reporters may work in pairs.

Movement

Members of the class work individually and move through the events of their day, leading up to and including the Fire. The events they show in movement are those which recur to them in a dream, so the quality of the movement might reflect this, and the sequence need not, anyway, be very long. Individuals might then be brought together to work as a group, or the physical statement might be followed by a story-telling session, in which they retell the events of the dream they have just moved through, either to a partner, or to the class as a whole.

STORYTELLING

One of the most valuable structures available to the drama teacher and one often used in the lesson examples is storytelling. This can provide the initial starting-point for the work, it can be a means of establishing what has already taken place, and it can be a way of bringing the work to a satisfactory conclusion. It is important to emphasise that drama is not to do with the re-enactment of stories already known, but with the building together of new stories. If the class are eager to re-enact a favourite story, it may be possible for the teacher to shift their thinking from the mere outline of the events to a consideration of the themes within the story. Merely to re-enact stories from books or television is unlikely to stretch the class in its thinking. The teacher has to find ways of approaching familiar material which will deepen the group's understanding of the original story.

A useful approach, especially with younger children, may be to stress that 'we are going to make up a new story — one that no-one has heard before.' The teacher needs the children to be in the story, and may be in the story herself. The teacher may already have decided the starting-point, or may ask for suggestions from the children about what should be included in the story.

The teacher as narrator.

In this example, the teacher started by telling a class of infants about a *very* big house, which was surrounded by a *very* big garden. Many people worked there, but not one of them had ever seen the owner of the house, and nobody knew who he was.

The class began to work at various tasks in the house and garden. The teacher called them back and asked whether anyone had seen the owner of the house. At last, one boy said that he had come across a giant in one of the bedrooms. The others accepted this idea, and elaborated it, so that it became clear that the giant was wicked and ate people. Was it possible to go on working for such **The teacher has to make the killing of the giant significant.** a wicked giant? The class decided that they would kill him, and didn't seem to think that this would present them with any problems. The teacher asked them to draw a picture of what they thought the wicked giant would look like.

Re-telling of the story to establish what has happened and to move it on.

When the drawings were finished, the teacher told the class the story from the beginning, to the point where the villagers were discussing how to kill the giant. 'Suddenly, the villagers heard a knocking at the door.'

Teacher in role.

At this point, the teacher ceased to be narrator, left the story-telling circle, and stood outside the group. The class grew excited and nervous, and began to think about hiding. Eventually, the teacher, in role, asked, in a worried way, 'May I come in and talk to you?' The children agreed, but were rather apprehensive. Maybe she was the giant! The teacher came in and sat down. 'You've found out about the giant, haven't you? And what are you going to do about him?' 'We're going to kill him!' The teacher was very upset. 'Oh, dear, it's worse than I thought. You see, I'm his mother.' The children were very taken aback. It was obviously not going to be so easy to kill a giant who had a mother. Was there any way they could persuade him to be less wicked? At length it was agreed that if they were each to make him their favourite food, he might be persuaded to give up eating people.

The children each prepared something for the giant to eat in mime, and gave it to the giant's mother, after describing it to her.

Since time was running out, the teacher told the story, from the beginning again, but now including the latest developments. Then she told them what happened when the giant's mother gave the giant all the food prepared by the children — ice-cream, sausages, candy-floss, chips, fudge, beans, and so on — and how he reacted. At last he was completely reformed, and all the people went back to work in the very big house and the very big garden.

The ability of the class to use narrative effectively themselves can be of great use within the drama, e.g. in describing their encounter with the giant, their bravest deed or greatest adventure, or how they received their tribal name. The following exercises may prove useful in promoting the pupils' confidence in their ability to make a sustained verbal contribution to the drama, and developing their skill in language use.

Sharing the Story

The teacher tells an improvised story and pauses every so often. He points to someone in the group to add an appropriate word: 'Once upon a time there was a young . . . He walked until suddenly . . . He said . . .'

This exercise can be very good training for the teacher in thinking on his feet, and using the ideas of the class. Eventually, he should be able to hand over most of the story to the group.

Moving and Narrating

The teacher asks the class to imagine they are about to start on a great adventure. It is midnight, and they are standing outside a castle, or an enchanted forest, or a modern tower block, a prison camp, or some other suitable location. They must enter this place, to accomplish some vital deed. They need to decide who they are — heroes, spies, murderers — and to possess all the attributes of such a character. Their journey will be beset with dangers and difficulties. Individually, the class sets off on their various quests. When the quest has reached its moment of greatest tension, each person freezes.

The teacher may add lighting and sound effect, to heighten the tension.

Now, in pairs, the class tell each other the story of their adventure. It has become even more exciting in the telling, and the difficulties are exaggerated, as are the courage and resourcefulness of the teller. Pairs and groups can be added together, so that eventually some pupils are talking to quite large numbers of others.

If all the class do not finish at the same time the teacher may stop the exercise at any point.

The physical moving-through of the experience before the narration seems to make it easier for the pupils to visualise the events, and select and shape the narrative.

Narrators and Actors

The class sit in a circle.

The teacher chooses two narrators, who share the story between them. One tells a short portion of the story, then hands it over to the other person to continue, but takes over again after a few minutes. The rest of the group become the characters and objects in the story, and act it out silently. Their participation may influence the shape of the story.

This game can also be played with the narrators providing the story as before, but the actors adding the speech for themselves.

Life-stories

In pairs. A has completely lost his memory. B knows everything that ever happened to A, and recounts the story of his life to him, which can be as full of incident and drama as possible, but should end on a hopeful note. It is important that A should not question or challenge B, but that B should be able to deliver a monologue without being interrupted.

These exercises can be very useful in training children to listen to each other and respect each other's ideas.

Then change over.

To give a group practice in using sustained narrative, one can set up story-telling occasions — e.g. Robin Hood and his band of outlaws recall their most famous escapades. A league of the greatest spies and secret agents meet once a year to recount their greatest exploits. The tribe tell stories of the deeds of their ancestors and the legends of the tribe.

TEXT AND DRAMA

Text can be a starting-point for improvisation, and improvisation can lead to a close study and deeper understanding of the original. This approach is particularly useful in the upper part of the secondary school, where the need to study texts for examination purposes often deadens appreciation. Lower down the school, and at primary level, it can be a means of releasing children from the tyranny of the script, and allowing them to examine the themes within the text they have been given. Improvisation becomes a tool for the exploration of the ideas, relationships and language of the original text.

Where the broad outline of the original is known, movement is an economical way of isolating and defining relationships.

These spatial relationships can also be used as the starting-point for an improvisation.

A class of 5th formers, studying Macbeth, were asked to choose the scene which they felt to be central to the play, and to move through it silently, emphasising the bearing of the characters to each other, and spatial relationships between them, and how these relationships changed in the course of the scene. They chose the banquet scene, and used the whole group to stage it. A strong sense of ritual and hierarchy became apparent, as well as the alteration in Macbeth during the scene, and the contrast between the opening of the scene and the hurried and undignified exit of the guests.

Role-play in pairs or small groups can illuminate the text, and may be particularly useful where the language of the original presents obstacles to understanding. One of the easiest approaches is to develop modern parallels to the scene which is being studied. The following brief examples indicate some of the possibilities:

In pairs:

This kind of approach should lead directly to a consideration of the appropriate scene in the original. King Lear

Othello

A has an older relation, B, staying with them on an extended visit. Now, B's presence has become a nuisance, and A wants B to move out. But, since B is wealthy, how does A suggest this without offending B?

A is jealous of B's friend or wife, and tries to influence B against them, without being directly unpleasant. B admires and trusts A.

In threes:

King Lear

A and B vie with each other to impress C, who is an influential older person, perhaps a relative, with money.

In fours:

Romeo & Juliet

A, a young girl, introduces B, her boyfriend to her parents. There is a very strong reason why they do not approve of B — perhaps his past behaviour, his prospects, his race or religion.

Particular scenes in the play can be extended either onward or backward in time, to develop scenes which the dramatist has not provided:

Hamlet

How does Gertrude behave to Claudius when she meets him after her interview in the bedroom with Hamlet?

Macbeth

What happens to Lady Macbeth just before she commits suicide?

Another way is the 'Upstairs, Downstairs' approach, where events in the text are examined from the point of view of the servants and minor characters:

Romeo & Juliet

How does the Nurse talk about Juliet when she is with the other servants, and what is their reaction to her?

How do the servants in Macbeth's castle react to the news of Duncan's murder? Will Macbeth's elevation to the throne affect them?

Macbeth

What do the servants in Othello's household think about his marriage to Desdemona, and his subsequent behaviour?

Othello

When the text is very well known, perhaps when it is being studied for an examination, it is possible to work more deeply.

A pupil can adopt a particular character, and be questioned in role by the rest of the class. Here, the questioning should not merely check on the pupil's knowledge of the facts of the play, but ought to allow for individual insights and interpretations. The rest of the group may use their knowledge of the text to challenge the person who is in role, or may themselves take on a role in order to question or argue more closely:

Gertrude is questioned about her hasty re-marriage, and her attitude to Hamlet.

Hamlet

An inquest is held on Duncan. Both the Macbeths are called to give evidence.

Macbeth

Goneril and Regan are questioned about their behaviour to their father.

King Lear

Hamlet is examined by a number of psychiatrists.

Hamlet

These short passages can also be used as the starting-point for the pupils' improvisation.

The actual words of the original can also be investigated, to see what atmosphere and implications they contain, and how they are capable of a number of interpretations. Here, a very short passage should be selected, perhaps an exchange containing five or six lines. The pupils, working in small groups, can decide how they want to stage the piece, and what interpretation they wish to give the words. The spatial relationships between the characters, their inflections, the volume they use, will all be seen to affect the meaning. At first, in order to achieve very different interpretations, there may be a comic exaggeration of tone and gesture, but this should give way to an understanding of the variety of interpretation which the text will bear.

It is not only dramatic texts which can be approached in this way. Novels, documents, even pictures, will provide material for similar kinds of work.

'Romeo and Juliet' as a television programme

Shakespeare, Chaucer and other writers whose language is unfamiliar, may be approached by isolating the area the teacher wishes to explore, (e.g. the character of King Lear, the sequence of events in Macbeth), and setting up a documentary or news style of television programme where the pupils are thrown back on the text for the information they need in preparing and presenting their programme. Video and tape recording may be used as both a control factor and also an end product. This lesson is an example of the methods used by one teacher working with pupils who are studying the text in class for examination purposes with other teachers. The lesson is a 'one off' session and not part of a regular drama programme but the way of focussing on a text may be useful for studying any kind of material at both junior and secondary level.

Stage One

The class and teacher together isolated some of the subjects that they wanted to present. They suggested: 'Drugs being readily available to young people'; 'Violence in the streets of Verona'; 'Attitudes to marriage'; 'the social scene of the Capulet Family'; 'the church's attitude towards Friar Lawrence's behaviour'; 'Vendettas'.

Teacher as questioner/ facilitator suggested a 'news-review' as being the nearest approach to the ideas being put forward.

Stage Two

The beginning of the work was hesitant, as the teacher had not explained sufficiently well that she did not want a 'script'. However, each group discussed well and began to form a very clear idea of presentation. One group needed a cast of epic proportions to do the 'Capulet' party interviews and it was decided to limit the number of guests actually before the camera and use everyone else as 'crowd'.

Small groups formed, each taking one subject. They were given a time limit and writing material and asked to devise a five minute item.

Stage Three

The groups now had a more severe limitation on their work and this forced them to focus on what was really relevant or important. They did not seem to need reminding to go back to the text. The 'violence' group rehearsed. The 'drugs' group asked for additional material and information.

Teacher worried about the amount of time taken up and hurried round from one group to the other suggesting that they appoint a camera operator, a director and either interviewers or cast as needed.

This stage was useful in providing two things — a limitation to prevent excessive and irrelevant 'dramatic action', and an activity to prevent self-consciousness in presentation, but it could well be left out if equipment (sound or video) were not available.

Teacher as studio manager only concerned with technicalities. All 'artistic' decisions made by directors and camera people. Anyone not involved in that item watched the monitor. Silence was necessary for the recording.

Each item lasted only about 2 minutes with exception of 'violence' scene which was about 4 minutes.

Stage Four

There was a real camera available.

The 'Studio' was hidden behind screens up to this moment. The screened area was now opened and the directors and camera operators settled on shots, cues and 'visuals'. The groups were kept so busy making their programme they did not worry about the fact they they did not normally 'do drama'.

Stage Five

Each item was put into a running order and the programme was put together a bit at a time. Scenes were improvised. A group of Verona toughs interviewed, Escalus summed up. A tearful nurse was rather coolly handled by a very professional interrogator. The Capulets' high-living friends were sent up in a comedy scene.

Follow-Up

The whole tape was shown to the class. The quality of filming was bad but the teacher asked the class to think of themselves as critics and that they were either (a) to write a critical review of the programme's content and presentation; or (b) to write a publicity item for Radio or TV Times. (This was assessed by the English teacher at another lesson.) A discussion of the omissions and areas of guesswork followed, taken by both Drama and English teachers together.

The end-product was seen by teachers as unimportant but this was not true of the class; it was necessary to have some kind of resolution in terms of writing, to go back over the learning stages at the beginning of the lesson. By being critical of content the class could forget about how funny so-and-so was as interviewer. If video had not been used and the presentation had been done to the class direct, this might have been avoided, but focus and concentration might not have been so strong.

Kes

The class were reading the book for examination purposes, the language ability in the class was mixed and therefore reading and writing levels were also uneven. One English teacher wished to ensure that the boys could see a relevance in the book to their own situation. The drama teacher offered to take the class in the normal English period and they isolated one episode: 'Having cigarettes in school', as a simple drama lesson to extend some of the issues. The class had not done much drama before.

This first stage was necessary with this class in order to prevent any kind of sending-up of well-known personalities on the school staff. In any other circumstances it could go straight into next stage, i.e. class improvisation.

Stage One

The class first acted as audience. The drama teacher played a shopkeeper. The English teacher played a schoolboy buying cigarettes out of school, a visitor to the class played the teacher. The audience could at any moment 'freeze' the action and could question one or other character as to their motives. Other characters could be asked to block their ears.

During this scene the teachers asked a few questions to try to add something they saw as relevant, otherwise no activity on their part except listening.

Stage Two

Second scene. The boy was taken to the headmaster. The class now took all the parts themselves. They were serious and concentrated. The questioning became quite profound. At one stage they needed to know what the parents' attitude might be and so extra characters were brought in. (No fooling occurred even though the boy answering for the mother was nervous and anticipated being laughed at.)

The English teacher led this discussion to bring it directly to the parental and teacher roles in the book.

Stage Three

The scene ended. A short discussion followed but not much was needed because of the simultaneous questioning and subsequent analysis. The class then read the passage describing the headmaster's study from the book.

The technique of 'freezing a scene' and questioning the characters is effective and simple. It helps the audience to become part of the activity and it deepens the participants' understanding of action and relationships. The questions can be as simple as 'why did you do that?' but imagine what the possible answer might be if it were followed through! Naturally, this technique does not have to be used in connection with text alone and it is interesting to note that the participants are 'speaking as' the people involved, not trying to 'act'.

PLAYMAKING

Playmaking using the children's own ideas does not necessarily imply presentation before an audience. It is simply that a sequence of lessons may build up into a piece of work that the class may want to 'finish off' with a certain attention to detail. They may also need to return to certain ideas and alter them in order to bring them into line with later work. It also enables the class to look at narrative and dramatic structure in a critical way. The following work may serve as an example of the structuring of a sequence of lessons, and the development of a theme. It is playmaking at its most simple and basic, with a class of 42 2nd Year Juniors.

The Kingdom of the Birds

Lesson 1. Classroom

The class saw an educational film which caught their imagination. It illustrated bird movement in flight, swimming, feeding, etc. As they talked about the film, the class began unconsciously to imitate the movements which they had seen. Birds were categorised and movements noted and imitated deliberately. Spontaneous demonstrations were given. These reactions gave the teacher an idea for a movement lesson.

Lesson 2. Hall (Mozart — 'The Magic Flute')

The children tried out 'flight patterns' in movement, following different leaders, changing pace and direction. Migration was mentioned, and a 'flight' of children organised. The necessity for leadership was discussed and explored. Reasons for migration were looked at.

Lesson 3. Classroom (Hans Andersen's 'The Swallow')

The children began to tell stories about migration. They were not very original, but the idea of one bird missing the migrating flock came up, and the question of how cold a bird might be without dying suggested the idea for a play. The class asked if they could follow this idea in the next drama session. The beginning of the play, about two children who find a frozen bird, was decided.

Lesson 4. Hall (Vivaldi — 'Winter' from 'The Four Seasons')

The class listened to the music. They selected a passage and worked out how they would have to represent the frozen world themselves, as they had no other resources. They ran, and 'froze', then imagined what it would feel like to 'unfreeze' (pins and needles, cramp, etc.) Speech was introduced, and an Old Woman picking up sticks who begins the story when the children meet her.

Lessons 5, 6, 7, 8

The class evolved a play, little by little, whenever the hall was available. Since more than 40 children were involved, and hall-time was limited to short periods, they had no audience and there was not a great deal of space. The final story was perhaps somewhat trite and had moved a long way from its source, but it possessed certain advantages, the chief among them being that it was the pupils' decision and responsibility, at any time, to continue or not as they chose. Presentation of the piece was simply seen as the natural development of the work, like pinning a painting up on the wall.

Many things are tried out and no-one is hurt if, finally their idea is rejected, since there is an air of great seriousness about the logic of each step and the necessity of a firm structure.

Normally the class wore vests and pants for drama as the school associated it with music and movement.

For the presentation the 'birds' used pleated skirts worn over their shoulders as 'wings'. Some of the 'kingly' birds had masks. The Mackintosh Monster was made from several fathers' raincoats buttoned together, with boys underneath. Thus it had several arms, each with over-large, men's gloves on.

The Plot that finally evolved

In the frozen country some children are walking, when they find a 'frozen' bird. They warm the bird and bring it back to life. An old woman who chances to come by tells them that a charm may be made by obtaining a tail-feather from the king of the birds and placing it upon a frozen pool. She cannot tell them where the Kingdom of the Birds is. The little bird is sure that the migratory flight of other little birds will help, if they can meet up before they have left. It may be too late. They find the small birds about to leave. The birds weave a net and fly with the children. Many adventures later, having defeated the monster, the children are conducted by the secretary bird to the court of the Proud Birds, where, at first, they meet with derision but argue their case, obtain the feather, and, escorted by all the birds, they arrive in the frozen country. The feather flames up, the ice begins to melt. Strange forms, in thawing reveal themselves as living things who dance in a spring ritual of re-birth.

INDEX